How to
Go to College
on a
Shoe String

The Insider's Guide to Grants, Scholarships, Cheap Books, Fellowships, and Other Financial Aid Secrets

By Ann Marie O'Phelan, M.F.A.

HOW TO GO TO COLLEGE ON A SHOE STRING: THE INSIDER'S GUIDE TO GRANTS, SCHOLARSHIPS, CHEAP BOOKS, FELLOWSHIPS, AND OTHER FINANCIAL AID SECRETS

Copyright © 2008 by Atlantic Publishing Group, Inc.
1405 SW 6th Ave. • Ocala, Florida 34471 • 800-814-1132 • 352-622-1875–Fax
Web site: www.atlantic-pub.com • E-mail: sales@atlantic-pub.com
SAN Number: 268-1250

ISBN-13: 978-1-60138-020-3   ISBN-10: 1-60138-020-8

Library of Congress Cataloging-in-Publication Data

O'Phelan, Ann Marie, 1960-
  How to go to college on a shoe string : the insider's guide to grants, scholarships, cheap books, fellowships, and other financial aid secrets / by Ann Marie O'Phelan.
       p. cm.
  Includes bibliographical references and index.
  ISBN-13: 978-1-60138-020-3 (alk. paper)
  ISBN-10: 1-60138-020-8 (alk. paper)
  1. Student aid--United States--Handbooks, manuals, etc. 2. College costs--United States--Handbooks, manuals, etc. I. Title.

  LB2337.4.O64 2008
  378.3--dc22
                                 2008007340

INTERIOR LAYOUT DESIGN: Vickie Taylor • vtaylor@atlantic-pub.com

Printed in the United States

Printed on Recycled Paper

We recently lost our beloved pet "Bear," who was not only our best and dearest friend but also the "Vice President of Sunshine" here at Atlantic Publishing. He did not receive a salary but worked tirelessly 24 hours a day to please his parents. Bear was a rescue dog that turned around and showered myself, my wife Sherri, his grandparents Jean, Bob, and Nancy and every person and animal he met (maybe not rabbits) with friendship and love. He made a lot of people smile every day.

We wanted you to know that a portion of the profits of this book will be donated to The Humane Society of the United States. *–Douglas & Sherri Brown*

The human-animal bond is as old as human history. We cherish our animal companions for their unconditional affection and acceptance. We feel a thrill when we glimpse wild creatures in their natural habitat or in our own backyard.

Unfortunately, the human-animal bond has at times been weakened. Humans have exploited some animal species to the point of extinction.

The Humane Society of the United States makes a difference in the lives of animals here at home and worldwide. The HSUS is dedicated to creating a world where our relationship with animals is guided by compassion. We seek a truly humane society in which animals are respected for their intrinsic value, and where the human-animal bond is strong.

Want to help animals? We have plenty of suggestions. Adopt a pet from a local shelter, join The Humane Society and be a part of our work to help companion animals and wildlife. You will be funding our educational, legislative, investigative, and outreach projects in the U.S. and across the globe.

Or perhaps you'd like to make a memorial donation in honor of a pet, friend, or relative? You can through our Kindred Spirits program. And if you'd like to contribute in a more structured way, our Planned Giving Office has suggestions about estate planning, annuities, and even gifts of stock that avoid capital gains taxes.

Maybe you have land that you would like to preserve as a lasting habitat for wildlife. Our Wildlife Land Trust can help you. Perhaps the land you want to share is a backyard— that's enough. Our Urban Wildlife Sanctuary Program will show you how to create a habitat for your wild neighbors.

So you see, it's easy to help animals. And The HSUS is here to help.

THE HUMANE SOCIETY
OF THE UNITED STATES.

2100 L Street NW • Washington, DC 20037 • 202-452-1100

www.hsus.org

Dedication

The book is dedicated to the one who keeps me going, my wonderful son Justin. For W. Paul Brown for all his love and support. For my mother Mary Louise O'Phelan for helping me start college in the first place. For brothers Michael, Daniel, Patrick. John, and sister Theresa — who all made it through college. For my father, John, I know you would have been proud. To all of my extended family and loved ones.

Table of Contents

Foreword

By Alex Fisher

When dreams of college are envisioned by parents and students alike, they often picture the intellectual adventure and engaging environment. These dreamers though are faced with the reality of the record-high expenses associated with higher education. The tuition is just one factor in the ever-growing list of expenses that no college student can be without. Parents must decide between the benefits of private versus public universities, housing, meal plans, technology purchases, and more. Students must also remember to be responsible with their parents' investment and use their time wisely.

There is no good reason to overpay for anything when a little research and guidance can help make the burden of paying for college more manageable. This concept rings true whether you choose to pay out of pocket, compete for scholarships, or take out student loans. This book will serve as your guide for not just a frugal college education but one where a few simple tips can save hundreds if not thousands of dollars.

You can purchase new books from the college bookstore, or get the same used book on the Internet for up to 75% off sticker price. You can purchase a new laptop computer for $1800 from your local electronics store, or one on eBay for a thousand dollars less. You can pay the high fees for residence at a dormitory or share an apartment with friends. The financial benefits of all the latter choices far outweigh the minor sacrifice in comfort. Living on a shoestring budget means to watch your daily spending and making wise financial choices when the time arrives. There is no more excuse for losing out on free money because of a lack of knowledge. This book will be your personal guide.

I leave you with the suggestion to absorb the details of this book and innovate with your own ideas to make your college experience a thrifty yet unforgettable one.

Alex Fisher
Owner of Crown Tutoring, LLC
www.crowntutoring.com
215-825-8522

CROWN
TUTORING
In-Home Tutoring Specialists

Alex Fisher is the owner and CEO of Crown Tutoring, LLC, a nationwide in-home tutoring agency. Mr. Fisher is also pursuing his medical degree at the University of Medicine and Dentistry of New Jersey's School of Osteopathic Medicine and he graduated Summa Cum Laude in Biology with Honors from Georgia State University. He balances his responsibilities as a medical student along with his role as the owner and chief decision-maker at Crown Tutoring, LLC. He began as a tutor throughout college and now employs local teachers to provide superior one-on-one tutoring in all subjects and grade levels throughout the U.S.

Preface

By now, we all know that the cost of getting an education is soaring. College Board, a not-for-profit membership association whose mission is to connect students to college success and opportunities, states in their report "Trends in College Pricing 2006:"

> The average rate of tuition at four-year private colleges was about $21,235; four-year public universities average $5,491. And not only that, the costs keep going up, as College Board has also found that...most students and their families can expect to pay, on average, from $95 to $1,404 more than last year for this year's tuition and fees, depending on the type of college.

These days getting a college degree is vital to working in many fields, from nursing, to teaching, to engineering, and, even with the hefty price tag, getting an education makes good economic sense. According to a 2007 College Board study, education pays: "Over a lifetime, the gap in earning potential between a high school diploma and a B.A. is more than $800,000."

You have to figure out how to get the money for college in the first place. Yes, tuition and costs are rising, but there is good news: there is more than $134 billion in financial aid available. There are low-interest loans, grants, scholarships, cooperative education, work-study programs, and more, all designed to help you get that degree.

So where do you start? The first thing you should do is apply for all the free college money that you can. Grants and scholarships can help, and their values can range from as low as $500 to assisting with covering the entire cost of college. Yes, the entire four years can sometimes be paid in full by a grant. Once the free money sources are exhausted, you should check out student loans. Student loans can provide you with low-interest loans and you will not have to worry about starting payments until six months after you graduate. That gives you plenty of time to find a job in your chosen profession and be in a position to make payments. Even if you are in a position to make loan payments, it is in your best interest to make them as low as possible. Lastly, there are other resources for money, such as home-equity loans, private loans, and retirement fund loans, but those should be considered only after you have exercised your other options, and you should seek the advice of a financial advisor before even thinking about it.

How to Go to College on a Shoe String: The Insider's Guide to Grants, Scholarships, Cheap Books, Fellowships, and Other Financial Aid Secrets is designed to help you find out what college funds are available to help you pursue your education, and how to get through college as inexpensively as possible from your first day of school until graduation. Chapter by chapter, you can explore what money and opportunities are available and how to apply for and receive the funds for your education — whether you are working on a two-year degree, a four-year degree, a master's degree, or even a doctorate degree. Plus, you will gain all sorts of tips and helpful information to stretch the dollars that you do have.

By cutting college costs in the first place, you will have that much less to pay back once you finish your education. And once the bills start rolling in, like the mortgage, the car payment, and your insurance, you will be glad you did everything you could to take advantage of college funds that were designed to help students pursue their education more affordably.

Introduction

While there are a lot of books out there designed to help you cut back on your education costs, *How to Go to College on a Shoe String: The Insider's Guide to Grants, Scholarships, Cheap Books, Fellowships, and Other Financial Aid Secrets* is one of the more comprehensive books on the market, and one of the most easy-to-follow. From providing you with the contact information for grants, scholarships, and loans to explaining all the steps you will be taking to win them, this book will guide you through the process of finding money for college from start to finish. Plus, you will pick up some great money-saving tips along the way.

How to Read This Book

There is a wealth of information in this book, so your best bet is to read the book from cover-to-cover. That is how to get the maximum value out of it. But if you are short on time and attention, you can read the chapters that you are most interested in.

For instance, if you are one of the one million students who have been home schooled and you are wondering about how that affects your college application, you will find helpful information in Chapter 1. Although home-schooled students enjoy a reputation as being well prepared for college, and they tend to score better on the SATs and other standardized tests than do regular students, colleges sometimes expect your home schooling to be well documented, which you can read more about in Chapter 1.

If you are wondering about the application process and what kinds of forms you generally need to fill out, and what paperwork you need to provide schools with, Chapter 2 will outline what to expect, from getting your transcripts, to gathering letters of recommendation, to preparing for your interview.

Say you have heard about the Free Application for Federal Student Aid (FAFSA), but you are not sure what it is. Chapter 3 spells it out for you and tells you how to apply. The FAFSA is a form that schools, government agencies, and many scholarship committees use to generate the Student Aid Report (SAR) to determine your financial need. This report determines how much money you are going to get for college.

Maybe you have already received a scholarship, but it did not cover enough of your costs. What do you do? Chapters 4 and 5 cover grants and loans that may offer the perfect supplement to your scholarship. Everything is covered in these two chapters to help you find the funding that is right for you — from specifics on how to apply for the funding to who is qualified to receive the funds.

Perhaps you have always "heard" about cooperative education (education that blends academics with hands-on work), but you were not quite sure what it is. Chapter 6 will explain it, and also give you information on how to pursue it so you can zero in on saving on college costs, while at the same time gaining work experience to help build your resume.

If you have attempted to navigate the scholarship jungle, then you must know that it can be complex and daunting. Chapters 7 and 8 concentrate on answering all of your scholarship questions, while providing helpful information on how to pursue scholarship funds — everything you need is right before your eyes, from writing an effective essay to where to look for those scholarship dollars.

Of course, you cannot trust everything you read, and there are scams out there designed to rip you off under the guise of helping you receive college funds. Chapter 9 outlines what to watch out for so you are less likely to be taken advantage of by unscrupulous companies looking to steal your identity or your dollars.

You may have received plenty of college funding from student loans, grants, and scholarships, but still you need to keep your spending under control. Chapter 10 is filled with helpful tips and ideas on how to cut personal spending and maybe even save a few dollars along with way.

Whether you are a freshman studying political science, a sophomore pursuing a teaching degree, a junior on your way to becoming a marine biologist, or a senior studying pre-law, you will find all the information you need to get the money that is available for you to finish your education, and you will find out how you can best put those dollars to work.

While the cost of getting an education is soaring, more money is available for students than ever before. Once you finish reading this book, you will know where to find that money and how to go about getting it more effectively. Again, you can zero in on the chapters that apply most to you or dive in and read the entire book. Either way, you will learn plenty.

What to Do Once You Finish This Book

You can read about getting education funding until you are blue in the face, but it will not do any good unless you take the necessary steps to apply for the money. Getting funds of any sort — from loans to grants to scholarships — takes some effort on your part. You may have to fill out an application, apply for FAFSA, write an essay, or prove that you have financial need. It may take you hours or days to prepare, depending on what it is you are applying for, but by cutting costs you are essentially paying yourself. Once the student loan payments come rolling in, you will be glad that they are so low, and that you did everything you could to make them as reasonable as possible.

1
How Am I Going to Pay for College?

Higher education has never been cheap, but costs have skyrocketed in recent years. According to the College Board, tuition increases have outpaced the cost of living for the last 20 years. For the 2006-2007 college year, tuition went up more than 6 percent, while the cost of living rose only 2.4 percent. The cost of food, books, housing, transportation, and other expenses has also risen. The good news is that with some research and effort you can bring your college expenses down to a level you can afford, or even have them paid for completely.

Once you have the money you need for college, and know how to spend it wisely to stretch every dollar to the max, you are ready. But before all of this can begin, you need to start with the basics. The first question is which college are you going to attend?

It is never too early to start preparing for college. To maximize your scholarship potential, you should not only keep your grades up, but also participate in a variety of extracurricular activities so that when the time comes to fill out applications you will shine. There are also inexpensive ways of knocking out course credits while still in high school. Advanced Placement courses, CLEP exams, and completing coursework at a local community college can pay off big by reducing the time you will need to spend at an expensive college. Since your time is limited, you need to weigh these options carefully to ensure that you finish high school with a well-balanced record, and you may be on you way to finishing your freshman year before you even leave home.

You also have other things to do. But if you have a goal in mind and work steadily toward it, you will be glad you did.

CASE STUDY: PHYLLIS REARDON

Phyllis Reardon, Life Coach

phyllis@coachphyllis.com

www.coachphyllis.com

Planning for Success

As a life coach I help people discover what they want in life and set goals to achieve success. The following helpful hints have been modified from my Goal Setting Workshop for Parents.

As you prepare to enter college, a new journey in your life, achieving success will be determined by how well you plan.

Goal Setting

Success in college takes planning and a big part of planning is setting goals. Goal setting is asking the question: What do I want from college? Once you know your goals, the next step is designing strategies or actions. Success comes when you reach the goals or outcomes you set.

CASE STUDY: PHYLLIS REARDON

Goal Setting Activity

Writing a term paper:

First create a schedule and break up the work in doable-sized pieces. Display this schedule on your wall, desk, or day planner as a daily visual reminder. Schedule the day of the week and exact time to work on the paper. Make a note of the grade you want to receive. Announce to family or friends when the paper will be complete; making your goal public can help create motivation for completion as it sets up monitors. There are 168 hours in a week — use them wisely. Goals need strategies; strategies define actions; action leads to success.

Your Future View

Did you know that the more clearly defined a picture you have of yourself in the future the more likely you are to reach it? This picture of yourself could be called your possible self, the person you want to be. But pictures are not enough; goals must be set and actions taken to be successful.

Your Future-View Activity

Create a picture of yourself by asking where you want to be in five years. What does it look like? What diploma or degree is hanging on your wall? Where are you working? Where are you living? What is your salary? What car are you driving? Now make a list of the necessary actions steps to reach this desired self.

College Knowledge

New experiences like entering college may cause feelings of uncertainty, worry, and even fear. One way to lessen these real concerns is to become informed. Knowledge is power; increase your power. Correct information always seems to dispel doubts, so research your college. Know what the rules and regulations are, check out your course descriptions and determine what is expected of you, check out parking permits, tuition payments, campus recreation/ social clubs. Know how the library system works. Know who to contact if faced with unforeseen obstacles. Check out advisor/mentor or buddy programs, help centers, and the student council.

Take control, search the Web, plan, and increase your college knowledge.

Success will happen but only if you plan.

Whose Job Is This?

Getting ready for college, if done right, is really an ongoing process that can last throughout your high school years. The workload increases tremendously your senior year, as you begin narrowing choices for schools, start completing application packets, and continue working on financial aid. Who is going to do all of this?

Hundreds of choices have to be made, big and small. The biggest are the choice of college and major, but there are countless decisions to be made about the details of financial aid, where you are going to live, and how all of this is going to be paid for. These decisions can create lots of stress for families as students try to assert their independence and parents try to retain control and do what they think is best. Your college process can go down in flames if you and your parents are totally at odds about everything from which college to attend to who is responsible for licking the stamps.

This needs to be a team effort, with rights and responsibilities on the part of both parties. You need to sit down together early in the process and spell out what each side expects of the other. Open communication is going to be the key to getting through this. The family relationship is changing, and as this process rolls along, parents can watch their child evolve into adulthood. Here are some points to keep in mind to make this step a smoother one.

- Ultimately, the choice of school and major should rest with you — the student. It is your life, and you are the one who is going to have to live with the consequences. Your parents' job is to offer advice and counsel. However, you have to consider their point of view. You need to remember that your parents have been out in the real world for many years, and they really do know more about making a living and the working world. Plus, if they are helping you pay, they may want to have more of a say in what you choose to study. For instance, they may help pay for a degree in graphic design, but not sculpture.

- Your parents should help handle the financial aid forms. Parents have the experience and knowledge about finances that you just do not have. However, this is a great opportunity for your parents to work together with you and teach you about how money works. Some parents might feel uneasy laying bare their financial picture, particularly if they have made some mistakes, like spending your college fund on cruises to the Bahamas, but keep in mind that you are about to go off on your own and are more likely to do well if you begin to understand how family finances operate.

- Beginning in the senior year, if not before, you and

your parents are going to start accumulating forms and documents for college admissions, scholarships, and financial aid. These responsibilities can be divided; for example, you could be responsible for admissions and scholarship forms, but your parents could assume the role of supervisor and make sure everything is on track and deadlines are met.

- Even if you win lots of financial aid, there may be unmet costs. Make it clear who is going to pick up the tab, and for what amount. Do your parents expect you to get a part-time job while in school to take care of daily expenses, or are they willing to provide an allowance? Are you going to take care of clothing and automobile expenses or are your parents? Who is going to pay for the plane tickets at Thanksgiving and Christmas?

- Make it clear who is responsible for paying off those college loans that you are more than likely going to have to incur. Since you are going to benefit from a college education in terms of a higher salary, you should be the one to pay off the loan. However, some parents want their child to start out in life debt-free, and they have the means to take on this burden. If this is the case, your parents should consider withholding this offer until graduation. It might be sneaky, but if you feel that you have a big financial stake in doing well and landing a good job, you are likely to work harder and be more responsible about the choices you make in school. Whichever way your family decides to go, make sure everyone knows from the outset who is responsible.

By sharing the load you can keep peace and harmony in your household throughout this process. When the stress level rises, and deadlines are looming, and it all seems overwhelming, everyone should keep in mind that the ultimate goal is to get you the best possible start in life. It is all going to be worth it.

Going It Alone

The whole financial aid process assumes that parents are helping you along every step of the way, and that they are going to foot a large portion of the bill. Of course, this is not the case for everyone. Students come from every conceivable family situation, and the aid process just is not equipped to deal with all of them. Some parents refuse to help, some parents are not able to help, and some parents are in jail or hanging out at a Tibetan monastery finding themselves. If you are in one of these situations or something similar, you are obviously on your own, but unfortunately the financial aid process may not see it that way.

As far as financial aid is concerned, you can declare yourself to be an independent student if you are at least 24 years old by December 31 of the award year, you are married as of the date you file for financial aid, you are a military veteran, you are an orphan or ward of the court, or you have a child for whom you provide at least 50 percent support.

The financial aid office at your college also has the authority to declare you an independent student, but you are going to have to demonstrate very unusual circumstances. If your parents are both in jail, hospitalized, institutionalized, or if they have just plain abandoned you for some reason, be prepared to document this circumstance and produce reliable witnesses on your behalf, such as a clergy member or social worker, if necessary. Being an independent student generally makes you eligible for more aid, since only your income is being counted toward your ability to pay. However, individual schools may have tougher criteria for independence than the federal government, because it is in their interest not to grant this status. Even if you are declared to be an independent student, come colleges require that parents complete the FAFSA anyway.

What if your parents have money, are not in jail or a mental institution, but still refuse to contribute one dime toward your college education? This situation is rare, but it does happen. Some parents believe that their children should make their own way in this world, which includes making it through college without any financial support from them. This might build your character, but the bad news is that the financial aid office is going to act as if your parents are contributing, and you are not going to get an extra dime. You are going to have to find other ways to fund your education, just as your parents want you to do.

What You Can Do to Get Ready

You are already doing the most important thing you need to do to get ready for college, which is learning all you can about the right choices to make. Getting the most out of financial aid opportunities and making the right choices requires arming yourself with information and getting a good plan together. You can change your plan as your needs change, but the important thing is that you keep moving toward your goal of getting the best college education possible as cheaply as possible.

There are many sources of information available. College course catalogs contain a wealth of information about potential schools. Pay special attention to costs and financial aid requirements and deadlines. School Web sites contain a wealth of information about academic programs, extracurricular activities, and campus life. You should know, however, that Web sites are most often a condensed version of the college's catalog, which has the important details. Web sites are fine for narrowing down possible schools, but if you plan to send in an application it is worth the time to get a catalog and read over it carefully.

The Internet offers a gateway to loads of helpful information, from SAT prep courses to little-known private scholarship opportunities. The Appendix contains a list of helpful sites, and you should glance at all of them.

You also need to get organized early on. It might be a good idea to keep a notebook to start jotting down notes about especially helpful information that you might want to review later. Get a calendar to keep track of admissions, scholarship deadlines, and important financial aid dates. You do not want to miss financial aid or scholarship opportunities because you turned in an application too late, and soon you are going to be keeping track of a hundred things at once.

Make sure you keep copies of financial aid forms and applications. If you are applying for numerous scholarships, having copies of work you have already done can save you valuable time and energy, and it can help you keep track of what you have completed so far. Also, there is always the possibility that a valuable form can get lost in the mail, the fax can fail to arrive, or the e-mail disappears into cyberspace. Do not be afraid to pick up the phone and make sure an important application has arrived. These disasters may not happen very often, but this is too important a process to leave to chance.

Once you have educated yourself about the opportunities that are out there, start putting a plan together that will help you achieve your goals. Start thinking about scholarship requirements and how you are going to meet them. Also, you should start thinking about the best ways for you to knock out course credits early.

Savings Plans

Putting money aside for a child's education is a great idea for parents. Many states now have savings plans offering tax benefits that carry on even while a child is attending college. Savings will reduce the amount of financial aid you are going to need, and most importantly, the amount of money that you may have to borrow.

There is a tricky relationship, however, between savings and financial aid. A mistaken belief is that savings is going to reduce the amount of aid you can receive, so you are better off spending the money and pinning your hopes on a big aid check. For example, if you and your parents have saved enough to pay for your entire college education, you are not going to receive the amount of aid you would have received if you had no savings at all. However, only a fraction is counted toward the expected family contribution. The financial aid process does not expect parents to put their entire life savings toward a college education for their children. What this means is that you can have enough money in the bank to pay for college, and you will still be eligible for financial aid. You are better off with money in the bank that is earning interest for you and providing tax benefits than if you have no money at all.

However, it is a bad idea to save money in your name. This will have a big impact on the amount of financial aid that you can receive, because it is counted among your assets and it is assumed that all of this money can go toward college expenses.

Any amount of savings is going to help, but the best and most practical plan is to start early and be consistent. For example, if parents manage to save just $25 every week from the time a child is born until he or she reaches age 17, at 5 percent interest the balance will be $34,839. If parents start saving when the child is older, they will have to make a bigger contribution to get that kind of payoff, but any amount that can be set aside for the future will pay dividends.

There are several ways to save money. You can simply place money in a regular savings account at a bank, but you probably are going to earn a low interest rate, and you will have to pay federal and state income taxes on what you do earn.

A better place to stash your college fund is a Section 529

plan. These plans are administered by states, so the rules and regulations vary from state to state. The money that is placed into these plans is tax-deferred, like IRA or 401(k) contributions, but the bonus is that qualified disbursements are not taxed either. This allows parents to get the most bang for the buck. Even if you do not think you can save very much, putting at least some money into such a plan will have a financial benefit.

Another way of paying for college ahead of time is through a Section 529 Prepaid Tuition Plan. The major benefit of this plan is that it allows you or your parents to lock in in-state tuition at public schools at current prices. If you purchase half a year's tuition, it will always be worth half a year's tuition, even five, ten, or fifteen years later. Of course, this plan will only be worthwhile if you actually do attend a public school in your state. But if that is what you want it can be a great way to avoid steep tuition increases.

Like the 529 savings plan, prepaid tuition is now counted as a parental asset, so you can still qualify for financial aid even if all of your tuition is already paid for.

If you have been saving for a few years now, you may have a Coverdell Educational Savings Account (ESA). These accounts, often called somewhat erroneously Education IRAs, were created under the Taxpayer Relief Act of 1997. Anyone — grandparents, friends, and cousins — can contribute up to a total of $2,000 per year to these accounts. These accounts are treated as an asset of the owner for financial aid purposes. In most cases, this will be the parent, but ownership will pass to you when you reach age 18, unless provisions were made for your parents to retain ownership. Unless that happened, the account will become your asset and could reduce your aid eligibility.

A disadvantage of the Coverdell accounts is that contributions are taxable, although withdrawals for higher education purposes are not.

Get a Job?

Should you get a job while you are still in high school and start socking away money for college? Although this sounds like the American way, and we all admire the student who works his or her way through college, the answer is no. Any income you earn over $3,000 is going to count against you and actually decrease the amount of financial aid you will be eligible to receive.

You are much better off spending your time studying, being involved in extracurricular activities, and preparing your plan for college. These things will pay off big in the end by maximizing your financial aid and scholarship opportunities.

Looking Good on Paper

Part of preparing for college is to think about how your record is going to look to admissions and scholarship committees. Admissions officers and scholarship committees do not know you. The only things they know about you are what courses you have taken, the grades that you have earned, and the extracurricular activities you have done. Since this is all they have to go on, you need to make yourself look great on paper. You might have the greatest leadership skills in the world, but unless you have actually held leadership positions in clubs or in school government, no one is going to know about it. Similarly, you might be a talented musician, chess player, debater, or you might have a driving passion for community service, but unless you can translate these skills and interests into some tangible accomplishments, your talents will go unnoticed, and your chances for scholarships will be scant. Competition for scholarships is going to be fierce, but if you have everything in place, you can bring home the money.

What to keep in mind to look your best on paper:

- Get copies of documents, awards, certificates, and other paperwork that proves that you completed, or were awarded, what you claim you did. Keep all of your paperwork together in a safe place, as you may need to refer to it again in your search for college funds, and even beyond when applying for work in your field.

- Get names and contact information of those that can prove that you did what you claim. For instance, if you do volunteer work at a local community center, keep track of where it was (name, address, and phone number), and who your supervisor was. Your supervisor may be able to help later on with a letter of recommendation, or he or she may be a great personal contact for future needs, such as job hunting.

- Keep your contacts up to date even if you are no longer involved in a club or organization. It is in your best interest to keep the lines of communication open with those that you may need to contact later. You never know when you may need their assistance, from providing you with work references to putting you in touch with someone that could help you in the future, such as a future employer.

Grades

Keeping up your grade point average (GPA) is an absolute must. It is how you will be compared to others, and it can make or break your scholarship chances. Even a small increase in your grade point average can make a difference of thousands of dollars. There are scholarships that do not consider grades, and we will cover those in a following chapter, but the safe path is to get good grades.

Good grades are one of the best investments in your future you can make. Some schools automatically hand out full scholarships to students with a certain GPA and SAT score. Even the schools that do not have full-ride academic scholarships often give a higher percentage of aid and a lower percentage of loans to students with high grades. Schools also give out merit scholarships regardless of need.

Keeping your grades up for four years of high school requires a commitment on your part, but even if you did not do so well in your freshman and sophomore years, you can still bring your average up if you are willing to work at it. Any increase will be worth the effort.

Do not take the easy way out by avoiding challenging courses. It might be easier to make high grades in easy courses, but scholarship committees will take one look at your transcripts and not be impressed. When choosing your high school courses, follow your high school's college preparatory guidelines. Also, look at what the colleges you are interested in require of incoming freshmen. Make sure you have covered all of the bases.

If you excel in a particular subject, such as math or history, make the most of it. Take the hardest courses in that subject your school offers and put forth your best effort.

SATs & ACTs

The SAT and/or the ACT are the most important tests you will take in high school. Every year there are calls for schools to rely less on standardized testing, but the reality is that the SAT and ACT are objective measurements schools can use to compare students from different backgrounds. Be sure to check your college's requirements on which test you need. Usually, it is only one or the other (your choice), but some colleges and scholarships specify which one.

Scholarship committees also rely heavily on SAT and ACT scores, because they are a convenient way of comparing students from different backgrounds. Many merit scholarships are based simply on the highest scores, and they do not even consider grade point average. Others combine SAT and ACT scores with grades. Either way, the higher your score, the better your chance of winning thousands of dollars.

So, an excellent way that you can improve your chances of getting into the college you want and getting it paid for is to make the best possible score on the SAT and/or the ACT.

If you are willing to invest four years of blood, sweat, and tears to keep up a killer GPA, why not invest six weeks to improve your SAT or ACT score? For students whose GPA is somewhat lacking, a high score is the single best way to overcome it.

Studies have shown that a test preparation course can increase a student's performance significantly. For everyone, this can mean thousands of dollars in aid. It can also mean the difference between winning a big scholarship and being the runner-up. Or, it could mean the difference between getting into a highly selective college and being left out in the cold.

Do some research before choosing a preparatory course. Some are expensive, while some are reasonably cheap. A prep course is an investment, so do not choose a particular course simply because it has a lower cost. Some achieve big results, and others can give you a more modest increase. What you want to look for is a big increase, because it could means thousands of dollars in scholarship money.

If you cannot find a course that is offered in your area, there are books available for purchase or in your local library that offer advice and practice tests. It is a good idea to consult these from time to time as the SAT or ACT approaches, even if you do take a prep course. These tests are that important.

There are also online sites that can help you prepare for these tests; for instance, College Board offers the SAT Preparation Center™ online at **www.collegeboard.com**, where you will find practice questions, practice tests, and other helpful information.

If you are still struggling with the SAT exam and worried about how to pass it with the highest score, or perhaps you are not a good test taker, you may want to consider a tutor who can offer you one-on-one assistance with your preparations.

Tests are important to pass with as high a score as possible, especially those that are designed for college entrance, such as the SAT and the ACT, and before every test you take you might want to consider the following:

- Prepare for the test. Study the materials beforehand. Do not wait until the last minute to do so.

- Try to relax and get a good night's sleep the night before your test.

- Read the test directions carefully.

- Read the questions carefully. If it is a multiple-choice test, look over every possible answer before deciding.

- Review your responses.

- Double check that you have answered all of the questions.

- Pace yourself.

CASE STUDY: CROWN TUTORING

Crown Tutoring

590 Lower Landing Rd., 87D

Blackwood, NJ 08012

Phone: (215) 825-8522

Fax: (323) 517-9991

CASE STUDY: CROWN TUTORING

www.crowntutoring.com

admin@crowntutoring.com

Alex Fisher, Owner

The higher SAT score you have, the greater chance you will have of receiving scholarship awards from private sources and schools. Plus, the better chance you will have at being accepted into the best schools in the first place. Your SAT scores are the equivalent to all of your years of hard work in high school — they are that important. Not only are SAT scores considered a preview of how a test taker will do in college, they have become a yardstick for measuring life potential. Not necessarily fair, but it is true.

You should start studying as early as possible for the SAT by using review books, but if you feel you need extra help, you should by all means enlist the help of an experienced tutor. It is worth every penny, as the payback for getting more financial aid, and a higher quality education, could be tenfold.

For instance, at Crown Tutoring you can receive in-home one-on-one tutoring, so you can learn in the comforts of your home. Experienced tutors are hired to help assist you with the SAT test with everything from learning about testing formats, to following test directions, to working on time management skills and taking short cuts that will help make standardized tests a breeze — whether it is the SAT, the MCAT, the LSAT, GRE, or GED that you are studying for. Crown tutoring will also recommend the necessary practice materials and will implement a study regimen, as well as administer practice exams and evaluate the results to make sure you are on your way to passing your SAT with the highest score possible.

An ideal college applicant will be well rounded with extracurricular activities, acts of citizenship, and leadership experiences, along with a solid GPA and high SAT Score. Admissions offices look at the whole picture, but the SAT score is part of their evaluation. Of course, the amount that is awarded depends in part on how well the student filled out an application, and how well they wrote an essay, and how much time they invested in searching for financial aid in the first place. So while you certainly need a good SAT score, you need to do the rest of the legwork as well.

By working with you to maximize your SAT score, you will have the extra edge you may need to get into the school that is first on your list, and increase your possibilities to receive more grants and scholarships. Ultimately that will lower how much you will have to pay back. The more well-prepared that you are for the SAT test, and the more comfortable you feel with test taking, the better you will do on this very important test.

Activities

Extracurricular activities can be difficult to choose. Many academically gifted students are loners who would rather have their nose buried in a book. Others would rather concentrate on their studies and feel that they do not have enough time to devote to anything else. All that is well and good, but when it comes time to complete admissions and scholarship applications and you are staring at all those blank lines, you are going to wish you had participated. Certainly, schools want motivated students who get the highest grades. But they are also looking for students with leadership or creative abilities, and students who are willing to devote some time to making the world a better place. They want to have a well-rounded student body, with students of all kinds of abilities and talents.

There are tons of opportunities, both within your school and out in the community, to get involved in something that interests you. One of the best ways of getting attention is to invent your own project. This shows initiative and leadership, two qualities that colleges are always looking for.

Should you devote all of your time to one activity, or get involved in as many activities as possible? The answer is both, but it might be difficult. You might be interested in only one area, such as sports, writing, or photography, or you might be the kind of student that likes to try different things, but not stick with one particular activity very long. You might be a combination of the two.

Scholarship committees and admissions officers are going

to look at both the range of your activities and the depth of your involvement, so it is better to have a mix to cover all of the bases. Find one activity that you enjoy and go for mastery. If you like chess, join the chess club, take part in tournaments, and become an officer. But also do other things, even if it is a small way.

Do not forget to look outside the school as well. Many students make the mistake of thinking that only school-sponsored activities will count, but this is not true. Almost anything you do, from ham radio to a local square-dance club, will count, and it will help show who you truly are. If you are interested in health care, volunteer at a local hospital or nursing home. You will pick up some useful skills, as well as beef up your applications. Even better, organize a volunteer effort to help at the local nursing home. You will get points for leadership as well as for community service.

If your activities are heavily weighted toward one area, do some simple and quick activities to broaden your resume. Your time is limited, and no one can do it all, so look for things you do in the community or school that will show your well-rounded skills.

Home-Schoolers

What can you do if you do not attend a regular school? The popularity of home school has exploded in recent years, and now more than one million students, or slightly more than 2 percent of all students, are home schooled. In 2000, about half of the nation's colleges had a formal policy on admitting home-schoolers. Four years later, more than 80 percent of schools had one. Admissions officials and scholarship committees have become accustomed to making decisions about students with alternative records. Home-schooled students also enjoy a reputation as being well prepared for college, and they tend to score better on the SATs and other standardized tests than do regular students. Admissions officials are well aware of this, but admissions policies vary by state, or even from school to school.

At some schools, you need to have all of the usual elements of a successful application. Harvard University, which does accept home-schooled applicants, requires letters of recommendation, SAT/ACT scores, SAT 2 scores from three subjects, a personal essay, and grades from any courses you have taken, which is the same that they would require of any student. The Massachusetts Institute of Technology has a similar policy.

Many schools are opening up the admissions process to better measure the alternative education that home-schoolers have received. The University of California at Riverside, for example, has recently adopted a policy that allows home-schooled students to submit a portfolio that details their coursework.

Talk to the admissions offices of schools you plan to attend by your junior year. Ask them what documentation they are going to require and what you can do to ensure that you will be accepted. Your school may have a policy in place, or they may be willing to work with you on an alternative application. The responsibility is going to be on you.

The big problem you are going to run into is that your mom or dad, or whoever has taught you, has given you grades for courses that only you took. In other words, there is no basis for comparison with other students, which admissions officers need in order to judge your worthiness. To put together a convincing application, you need to think about concrete ways that you can demonstrate your abilities so that they can be compared with others. Keep copies of tests you have taken, essays you have written, and research projects you have completed. This can show that you have learned the same material as public school students.

Of course, the most important thing you can do is to score well on the SAT. This is the most solid measurement that admissions and scholarship officials will have to compare you with others. If you can manage a near-perfect score, school officials are not going to care if were schooled at home, in Katmandu, or under a rock. You are going to get accepted and get financial aid and scholarships based on the scores alone.

You need to make friends with your local school system, because they can provide you with help. The guidance counselor can help when preparing for the SATs, finding and filling out scholarship recommendations, applying for financial aid, and completing many other tasks. You should also be able to take part in extracurricular activities like band, the school newspaper, or the academic team, if you so desire. Regulations on participation are handled locally, so you will have to do some negotiating. Start with the principal of your nearest high school. If you get no action, go next to the central office of the school system. If they will not budge, do not be afraid to take your case to the school board. Board members are usually elected community members, and they may be more sympathetic to your needs than school administrators. Plus, they have the power to change the rules.

If you do find that you are denied access to school activities, you need the fill the gap yourself. You do have the same opportunity as regular students to exhibit your leadership skills by spearheading community service projects or by finding other ways of demonstrating your leadership ability. Be sure that you can document these activities and the extent of your participation and leadership.

Also, you might be involved in an in-depth science or history project as part of your home schooling. These kinds of academic endeavors can help demonstrate your academic worth in lieu of grades. Keep copies of your schoolwork and projects in the event that you need to state your case in person before an admissions official.

Advanced Placement and CLEP

A great way to gain college credit while still in high school is through Advanced Placement (AP) courses or College-Level Examination Program (CLEP) exams. You can combine the two to get maximum punch.

Advanced Placement classes allow you to earn college credit for high school courses that you would take anyway. For example, instead of taking senior English and getting a course credit, take AP English and get the usual course credit plus the opportunity to earn college credit. The AP designation simply means that at the end of the course you can take a standardized exam for college credit. The College Board administers the AP program and testing. The higher your score, the more credit you earn. At this time, AP exams are offered in 22 different subjects, including biology, environmental science, calculus, music theory, physics, computer science, English, Spanish, government, and studio art. Ask your school counselor about which courses are offered at your school and at what times. The cost of an AP exam is about $84, which is a real bargain compared to the cost of tuition.

If your school does not offer the course that you are interested in, there are two ways around this problem. One is to take the course at another school. This may involve some serious time management, but it is doable. Another option is to study for the exam on your own. There are test preparation books available for the AP exams, just as there are for the SAT.

Be aware that these courses are designed to be taught at a college level, so they are going to move at a faster pace and cover more material than a regular high school course. In other words, do not try to do everything at once during your senior year. Take a couple of AP courses during your junior year and a couple more your senior year. If you make high scores on the exams, you could be granted a year's worth of college credit, and you have just cut your college costs by 25 percent. And you have gained high school credit to boot. Many teachers curve the grades so that your grade point average will not suffer just because you are taking a tougher course.

If you are not ready to take full advantage of this program, you can at least play to your strengths. If you excel in biology, then you are going to do well in AP biology. Do not pass on AP classes because you think they are only for the best students in your school. What it takes to succeed is effort, not genius. You are going to take these courses in a year or two anyway, so why not take advantage of an opportunity to get a head start?

Be aware, however, that not all schools accept AP credit, even though the huge majority of schools do. The ones that do accept AP scores generally will accept up to one year's worth of credit. Check with the schools you plan to attend just to make sure.

The College Board also runs the CLEP program, but it is much broader in scope than the AP. CLEP tests are for anyone, regardless of ages or educational background. Each exam offers between 3 and 12 college credits, which are accepted by more than 2,000 colleges across the country. Again, check with the schools you plan to apply to about whether or not they will accept these credits. Many schools accept CLEP credits only in certain subjects. Each exam costs $65, which, like the AP exam, is a real bargain. Exams are offered in a much broader range of areas than the AP, including such subjects as accounting, marketing, and human growth and development.

Both of these programs are excellent ways to slash your college costs significantly, and they are well worth the effort.

Community College Courses

Community colleges, and even four-year schools, are reaching out more than ever to nontraditional students. Courses are offered at branch campuses or online, and they are designed for evenings or summer. These are real college courses, so be prepared to devote the time and effort necessary to do a good job and keep up your grades. These will be the cheapest courses you are going to find, but keep in mind that since you are not a full-time student, you are not going to receive much financial aid. Also, keep in mind that time spent working on night or online courses is time spent away from your high school courses or scholarship searches. In other words, do not squander an opportunity to win a big scholarship so that you can knock out a few courses on the cheap.

These courses might work better for you in the summer, when you do not have the burdens of your regular schoolwork. Most schools have liberal admissions policies, so you might be able to take a couple of courses between your junior and senior years, and then a couple more between graduation and your first semester at college.

Another way that community colleges can save you money is the transfer trick. You can complete your first two years at an inexpensive community or junior college, and then transfer to the college of your choice to complete your degree. You can save many thousands of dollars this way, and you will still end up with exactly the same degree.

If you are considering going to a community college, keep in mind the following:

- Make sure that you check into articulation agreements that your community college might have with the four-year college or university that you are interested in. You want to make sure that your credits will transfer to your four-year degree.

- If you have a major in mind, you might want to look at several community colleges and see which one best prepares you for your ongoing education. For instance, if you are going to major in math, you would want to pick a community college that best prepares you with plenty of math classes.

- If you do not know what your future plans are in terms of degree choice, you might be best to choose an Associate in General Studies degree program, where you would study many subjects and work to figure out what appeals to you most.

- Even during your first few years of college, you should meet with an academic advisor at your school to help you determine your right course of action.

Wrapping It Up

Few students can do it all, but every student can at least do something to get prepared for college. The important thing is to set a goal and prepare a plan for reaching it. You can do many things while you are still in high school that will pay off big when it is time to pack for college. For instance, you can work on taking higher-level courses and increasing your grades, you can start your scholarship and grant search early, you can develop a savings plan, you can research potential schools, you can look into community colleges in you area, and you can have a heart-to-heart talk with your parents to see how much they would be willing to help out — even if it means letting you live at home. Planning for college takes time and effort, but you will be glad you did.

2

Applications

A s you begin your senior year in high school, it is time
to start gathering information on colleges you are
interested in and begin making choices. There are
many reasons to choose a school, from finding one that
offers your field of studies, to finding one that offers the
most reasonable tuition, to choosing one that is based on
the best location. This chapter will help guide you through
the process of choosing the right school so that you will be
off to a good start in life.

Choosing the Right College

You are about to make an investment in yourself. A good
place to research higher education is a comprehensive
guide to colleges, such as The Princeton Review's *Complete
Guide to Colleges* and the College Board's *Book of Majors*
and *College Handbook*. Also consult some of the rankings

guides, such as the annual special issues of *U.S. News and World Report* magazine.

Criteria for choosing a school are:

Does the school meet your educational needs? For example, if you are interested in the sciences, you should look at colleges that have strong science programs. If you are interested in marine biology, is there a lab to offer you real-world experience? If you want to study foreign languages, do they offer a semester abroad or a similar program? How qualified are the teachers?

How comfortable will you be in a particular school environment? For instance, schools sponsored by religious organizations may impose behavioral restrictions, extensive coursework in Bible studies, or mandatory church attendance during the week. A larger school offers anonymity and independence, while smaller schools are like small towns — everyone knows everyone. Large universities have a variety of majors, while smaller schools may offer your specialty.

Consider the school's reputation. Graduating from a top-ranked school can open career doors. Corporate recruiters and graduate school committees do take a degree from a prestigious school seriously. Of course, your own performance is going to carry a great deal of weight, no matter what school you attend, but apply to the best schools you can.

Will you be employable when you graduate? Check out the job placement record for your chosen major. Do graduates land jobs with the top companies in your field? How many graduates go on to get their masters, doctorates, or law degrees?

Are you willing to attend? Worst-case scenario: attend for two years and transfer.

Visit Campuses

Before you settle on one school, visit the campus for a couple of days. Since you are going to spend four years and make a considerable financial investment, it is a good idea to make sure it is right for you. Your first impression from a lovely Web site may dissolve when you meet the students, or your bad impression from the school's literature may change when you are on-site.

Before you arrive, prepare a list of questions that can help you decide if the school is right for you. Your list might include:

- How much can you expect to pay for rent and utilities for off-campus housing?

- Are part-time jobs available near campus?

- What is the availability and cost of public transportation, both off- and on-campus?

- Do other students look like those you want to spend your next few years with? Does it seem to be a close-knit community? What is the cultural diversity of the student body?

- Can you imagine yourself on campus? Does it feel right?

- Is there campus security available, especially for night classes? You might ask about the crime rate.

- What is on the bulletin boards and in the college papers? What kinds of topics are the students discussing?

- What does the campus look like? Is it clean or dirty? New or rundown?

- How large are the classes?

- What services does the school offer? Job placement? Academic advising? Internships?

- What is the quality of the teachers? What is their education level? Do assistants teach classes?

Cost

Should you receive financial aid to attend college, it is possible that a private school will turn out to cost the same as a state school. Apply to all schools that you like, and apply to every possible source of financial help. As a precaution, choose a fallback school, one where you are guaranteed admittance. It should also be affordable so that you can attend and get your degree should you get only a small amount of aid.

Calculating the Real Cost

Once you have narrowed your choices down and have some idea of where you are headed, it is time to face the reality of finances. How much is this going to cost you? This is where some careful thought and planning can save you some pain later on. Most people tend to underestimate the cost of college because they fail to include all of the expenses they are going to encounter. Check out the catalogs of colleges you plan to apply to in order to get the basic costs.

- **Tuition:** A big up-front cost is, of course, tuition. This is the money the college charges you to attend classes, and it is usually based on a semester or quarter hour, with a discount for full-time students. Remember also that tuition tends to increase about 8 percent a year, so if you are planning a couple of years in advance, adjust this cost accordingly.

- **Fees:** This can be a tricky one. Colleges charge a variety of fees for all kinds of services. If you plan to take many science courses, expect to pay lab fees. Parking fees vary widely. At rural colleges, where lots of parking is available, permits are cheap. However, at urban schools, where space is a premium, you might have to pay as much as $500 per year for the privilege of driving your car. You will also have to pay a health fee, which covers doctor's visits at the school's clinic. Be sure to read over carefully what the health fee does and does not cover. For example, you usually have to pay full price for prescriptions unless you have insurance.

- **Books:** College textbooks are notoriously expensive. Costs vary by course, but you can expect to pay $200-$300 per semester. You are also going to need notebooks, pencils and pens, a calculator, and the usual school supplies.

- **Living expenses (on-campus):** If you choose to live in a dormitory, living expenses are easy to figure. Just be sure to check if the meal plan includes weekends (often they do not) and calculate accordingly. Also, if you plan to stay in the dorms during the summer, there will be an additional charge.

- **Living expenses (off-campus):** These expenses can vary according to location. Guidelines might be available from the school you plan to attend, or from organizations such as the chamber of commerce of the city where the college is located. In any case, you should include the cost of rent, utilities, phone and Internet service, and groceries. You should also include any deposits you will have to pay, including those for utilities, which can be considerable for first-time renters. If you have a roommate, these expenses can be cut in half or more.

- **Computer:** These days, a computer is necessary. For the greatest flexibility, you should choose a laptop. You can take it with you to classes, to the library, home with you on the weekends or on breaks, or wherever you need. Most schools offer free computer labs that you can use, but the inconvenience generally is not worth it. When choosing a computer, you should get one with enough memory and speed to get you through four years of college. Do not skimp on performance just to save a few dollars, because it may cost you in the long run. Look for a processor with a speed of at least 2 Ghz and a hard drive with at least 120 GB of memory. You should also consider the cost of software as well, which is going to vary according to which major you choose to study.

- **Clothes and entertainment:** This is where a lot of your disposable income is going to go, but it can be difficult to budget. Ask your parents what they spend on your clothing per year to get some idea of how much you can expect to spend. You are also going to want to have some fun, and fun usually costs money. College towns have many opportunities for you to eat, drink, and be merry, but also many opportunities to leave you broke. Be sure to include some money for the occasional splurge.

- **Insurance:** Generally, your parents' health insurance will continue to cover you while you are in school, and if they have a family plan there is no additional cost to keep you signed up. If you are not covered, you should consider getting your own health insurance. Costs vary, and many colleges offer an affordable plan designed specifically for students.

- **Cell phone, cable TV:** You are probably going to be willing to pay for the convenience of a cell phone. It is actually a luxury, not a necessity, but everyone has become so used to carrying one around that they think they are a necessity. The same goes for cable TV. Chances are, your dorm room is going to have a commons area with a TV, but for most people having their own remote is as necessary as underwear.

- **Household items:** Even if you are living in the dorms, you are going to have to consider the essentials of daily life. You can probably bring some of this from home, provided your parents will let you, but be sure to estimate the cost of what you may have to purchase.

- Blankets, sheets, towels, and washcloths

- Appliances, such as a coffee maker, small microwave oven, and toaster (or toaster oven)

Add all of these figures, and try to think of anything else you might need, or anything else you will be doing that will require extra money.

These expenses can add up to a scary total that goes way beyond tuition, which is scary enough. It is better, though, to overestimate what college is going to cost, and to be prepared for it, than to underestimate and find yourself short of funds. If you know what you are going to have to spend, you can better set your financial aid goals.

It is important to do this exercise for each school to which you are going to apply. Costs vary widely, and you cannot assume that the price of a dorm room at one school is going to be same as the price at another. Many schools even charge different prices according to which dorm you end up living in.

Keep in mind, though, that there are many ways to cut these costs or at least keep them under control. The following chapters are full of tips for finding money and cutting expenses.

A good way to feel better about the cost of going to college is to consider the cost of not going to college. One of the practical benefits of education is that it increases your earning power. Considering that you are going to be out in the world earning money for about four decades, even a modest difference in annual income can make a huge difference in your life. According to the Census Bureau, in 1999 high school graduates earned $25,900, college graduates earned $45,400, and people with professional degrees earned $99,300. Over a lifetime, a college degree can mean more than a million dollars in extra income. In other words, in spite of the high cost of a college education, it remains the best investment you can make in yourself.

There are also many professions that require you to have a degree. Even if you end up doing something else with your life than what you studied in college, your degree is going to open doors for you your whole life that would otherwise remain closed.

CASE STUDY: CANDEE LYNN WILSON

Candee Lynn Wilson

"The Saving Lady"

4322 Botticelli St.

Lake Oswego, OR 97035

www.101WaysToSaveMoney.com

www.MySavingPlace.com

SavingLady@MySavingPlace.com

During my 64 years I have been a starving student, single parent, sole breadwinner, and self-employed — a recipe for a saving train wreck. My father was a hard worker, but his attitude toward money went something like, "If you cannot do something first class, do not do it at all." My mother, an extremely frugal-minded woman, was always bailing my father out of financial disasters.

CASE STUDY: CANDEE LYNN WILSON

Unfortunately, my mother never passed on to me her saving secrets. I was left to discover those by trial and error. I hope I can make a difference in someone's financial future by passing on what I have learned through my Web site and blog.

Following is some general saving advice that will not only get you through college but also the rest of your life.

- Consider a local community college for your first two years of study. You will pay much less for your prerequisite courses. If a community college is not an option, check into in-state or public schools where tuition will be substantially less than a private college or university, and entry requirements will usually be more liberal.

- School housing is a huge expense, so look at schools in your own community or in a different city or state where you have a friend or relative with whom you can make a living arrangement. You might not think it is cool to live with your parents or old-maid aunt during college, but you will come to appreciate the money it saves. Zip up your pride and you could avoid really big student loans.

- Plan on working part-time to defray costs. This means not loading up on credit hours that leave you no time for anything except study and play. A school/work/play schedule will teach you time management and prepare you for a point in the future when part-time work may just bail you out of a temporary financial jam.

- Learn to take public transportation, ride a bike, or walk. The cost of maintaining a car is a big drain on the pocketbook. If you must have a car, buy a good used one for little money, paying cash so you can minimize the cost of insurance by only carrying liability coverage. Even when you can afford to buy a car, always pay cash and never buy new.

- Look for used textbooks online at sites like **Amazon.com**, **Textbooks.com**, **Bookbyte.com**, or **Half.com/Textbooks**. When you are finished with them, go back and resell them online to recoup part or all of your investment. In the future, buying "recycled" furniture, clothing, household items, etc. is not only frugal but "green" as well.

Public versus Private

One of the options you will have to consider when choosing a school is whether to attend a private school or a state-funded college. There are advantages and disadvantages to each.

A private school diploma traditionally has carried more prestige than one from a public school. Recruiters and graduate school committees have also traditionally looked more favorably upon private schools. However, as with any degree, there are no guarantees. A fancy pedigree may not help you succeed. Also keep in mind that many state schools have established reputations as good as, or better than, private colleges. The so-called "public ivies" are often great bargains, even if you have to pay out-of-state tuition.

As always, before you decide on a school just because of its name recognition, do your homework. Consult the college ratings guides and make sure the reality matches the hype. You might find some surprises.

What private schools can do for you is offer options or alternative curricula that are not available at public schools. Small private schools are often founded with guiding principles or beliefs that set them apart. Smaller schools have also made themselves more attractive (and therefore competitive) by offering small class sizes, unusual course requirements, or interesting social programs. If you are the kind of person who likes to wander off the beaten track, then a private school somewhere can get you there.

The reason students do not consider applying to private

schools is that they are more expensive than public schools. Private schools are more affordable than you think. While their tuition costs may be higher, often private schools have more scholarships and grants to offer their students, and once you factor those into the bottom line, you may realize that a private school education may be more affordable.

There is also a way to obtain a prestigious private school degree without the expense of paying four years of private school tuition. You can earn two years of credit at an inexpensive public school, and then transfer to a more expensive dream school to finish your degree. You end up with the same diploma you would have received had you attended all four years. Be careful, though, to check out the school's policy on transfers. Most schools limit the number of transfer students they will accept, and require a respectable grade point average as well. There is no guarantee that you are going to get in, but this is an option for those who want the cachet a private school diploma can bring without the cost.

In-State versus Out-of-State

What if you choose the public school route, but the school you want to attend is in a different state? Many state schools have established excellent academic reputations that rival the best private schools, so if prestige it at the top of your list of criteria for choosing a school, this might be a worthwhile option for you. An out-of-state public school might also offer a certain program of study that is not available in your state. All of these are good reasons to leave home.

Be prepared to pay. Public schools are funded in part by tax dollars, so if you live in a different state you will be expected to pay this portion as additional tuition. Residency requirements vary by state, and most states have toughened up their policies in recent years.

Some top-notch out-of-state schools (also known as public ivies) are better bargains than others are. Tuition at the University of Michigan and the University of Vermont, for example, has become as expensive as private school for out-of-state students, at $35,000 a year, but other schools, such as the University of North Carolina at Chapel Hill, are relatively cheap by comparison.

If it truly is your dream to attend an out-of-state school, ask the school's financial aid office about residency requirements as early as you can, in case it might be possible for you to meet them. Some schools allow you to establish residency after you have attended for a certain period, but generally this involves living off-campus. You probably will also be required to file a tax return in that state, as well as register your car there. Before all this happens, be prepared to work extra hard to come up with additional funds.

Location Matters

The type of environment that the school is located in can have a great effect on the cost of your education. Rent tends to be high for schools located in urban areas. Schools that are located in smaller towns tend to have the lowest cost of living. If you plan to live off-campus and money is tight, this should be a real consideration in your choice of schools.

Location also has a big effect on your transportation costs. If you plan to drive home often, the farther away you are the more it is going to cost. If the school is too far away to drive, you will probably want to fly home several times a year, which can be costly, especially if the distance if far.

If you do not have or want to have to buy a car, you may want to consider what kind of public transportation is available. Check with the city's transportation department to see if buses are readily available and how often they run. You might want to see how often they come and go near your school. A few cities, such as New York, San Francisco, and Chicago offer the added bonus of being able to take trains and cabs, if you can afford them. Other commuting issues will be presented later in this book.

An additional consideration for location is climate. If you are accustomed to the sunny warmth of Florida, a Wisconsin winter is going to be a real shock. If you prefer a mild climate, then you are not going to enjoy the heat and humidity of South Carolina. It seems like a small consideration, but remember, you are going to have to live there for four years. Plus, if you do not have the clothing, then that is another consideration. If you live in a warm climate and do not have warm sweaters, jackets, boots, and mittens, that can add up to hundreds of dollars that you have to dole out just to go to college.

Living at Home

One of the best ways to cut the cost of attending college is to live at home. This option is not for everyone, of course. Some students do not live within commuting distance of a desirable college. Most students, though, simply do not want to live at home. Being on your own is part of the college experience, and is one that many students loathe giving up. There definitely are advantages to living on-campus or near school: friendships are easier to make and sustain, and you will feel more a part of the college community.

The main advantage to living at home is that your parents are probably footing the bills. You will pay no rent or dorm fees, utilities, or perhaps even food. If you do decide to face the situation and go it on the cheap, there are some hazards to watch out for. Although it may be cheap, living at home and going to school may not necessarily be easy.

If your parents are pressed for cash, you may want to consider working out an arrangement with them that you pay rent for living at their house. The rent, no doubt, would still be less than if you were out on your own somewhere else, and you can enjoy the comforts of home while pursuing your education.

Commuter Blues

Driving to school can be a real burden. Parking is the first problem. Most schools grow faster than their parking lot, which means when school begins in the fall you might find yourself driving onto curbs or parking your car in the street to make it to class, because there are no spaces available. The situation tends to ease in the afternoon and evening, when fewer students are in class. This schedule could take some getting used to, but it will relieve many headaches for you. An additional option is to take the earliest classes, which are also not very popular. This will get you into a parking space before the rush begins at 9 a.m.

Keep in mind that commuting to school is not free. First, with the price of gas at an all-time high, the daily drive to campus can get expensive. Estimate the number of miles you are going to drive each week, including weekend trips to the library, and calculate how much fuel is going to cost. Also, keep in mind that commuting is going to add wear and tear to your vehicle. You are going to do this for four years, so you are going to need regular maintenance such as oil changes, along with some major expenses such as a new set of tires. You are also going to need a reliable car to begin with. If your car breaks down during finals week, you are going to have to do a lot of explaining to your professors, who are not going to be very sympathetic.

With these words of caution in mind, commuting might still be the best option for you. Not everyone lives down the street from their dream school, but most people live within driving distance of at least one college.

Online Options

A way to avoid the commute to school is to take online courses. The number of Internet courses has exploded in recent years. They were originally designed for nontraditional students, because students who had full-time jobs and a family needed greater flexibility than on-campus courses could offer. Nowadays, even traditional students are signing on because of that same flexibility. The courses operate in a number of ways. Some courses require at least some contact with the professor in a classroom setting, usually at the beginning of the course. Thereafter, students do most of the work on their own, checking in with the professor and their class through an online chat room setup. Work can be assigned and turned in through the Internet. Testing varies. In some cases, exams have to be proctored by an approved person, while other courses require a trip to a real classroom, where everyone takes the test together.

If you are interested in completing much of your coursework this way, be sure to check out all of the course requirements thoroughly to make sure that you are not going to run into any problems. These should be listed on the course Web site, and you can always check with the professor to be sure. If you have research projects, you could end up spending so much time driving to the library or the lab that you might as well have taken on-campus courses. Your local public library cannot compete with a college library that caters to students by subscribing to specialized journals and ordering books and other research materials.

Also, you need to make sure that you have the motivation to get the work done on time without a great deal of prompting. Some students need the teacher's interaction to learn. Your ability to succeed in an online course may depend on the subject matter. If you usually have trouble with English or math, you may be better off in the classroom.

Also, you need to have a place to work free of distractions. Younger brothers and sisters, friends, and even parents can get in the way. A bedroom or an office that is quiet and isolated from all of the things going on in the rest of the house would be ideal.

An option that has become available in recent years is to earn an online degree offered by a for-profit college. A for-profit college is a corporation, like the University of Phoenix, that offers accredited degrees just as a nonprofit college does. These schools have catered to graduate students in the past, particularly for business degrees, but they are now moving into the undergraduate arena. Of course, check it the same as you would a traditional brick-and-mortar college. Pay special attention to financial aid to make sure they can offer you aid other than student loans. Find out about their graduation rates, and examine which companies actively recruit their graduates. Are they going to offer you the same job placement assistance that traditional schools do? Finally, make sure they are accredited in your major. Just because they are accredited to grant master's degrees in business does not mean that their social work program for undergraduates is also accredited.

You are likely to run into the same issues with online universities as you will with online courses offered by a traditional college, only more so. Your online school probably does not have a library, except what they have online. The Internet offers an incredible array of online journals and books, but it is still no match for a well-funded college library. Plus, if you are gathering several sources to work with, you are going to have a much easier time if you can lay everything out on the desk and put it all together. Working with multiple Web sites and writing a paper at the same time is awkward, to say the least. Brick-and-mortar libraries have one final advantage: well-trained and experienced librarians who can help you.

Also, you need to find out how many trips you are going to have to make to the main campus or corporate office. Depending on the school's location, transportation expenses can add up quickly. Frequent-flier miles are great, but not if the cost of airfare puts you out of school entirely.

Any way you choose to do it, getting online can be a hassle-free way of getting the coursework done. For commuters, it can make the college experience easier and it can provide some welcome flexibility throughout your college years.

Choosing the right college is more complicated than it sounds, but some effort now will pay off big in the end. Once you know where you are headed, and when you have a realistic idea of what it is going to take to get you there, you are ready to get the ball rolling.

To make shopping around for your online education easier, several search engines are designed to help you find the best opportunity for you to pursue your degree.

- Monster's Learning Network includes a source to help you find the right school, whether it is undergraduate, graduate, or post-graduate. According to them, "We provide information on prominent, accredited online schools and online degrees." To start your search, visit: **www.onlineschools.net**.

- Guidetoonlineschools.com is "an education directory specializing in online degrees, online schools, and distance learning." To start your search, visit: **www. guidetoonlineschools.com**.

- Directory of Schools assists students who are seeking online degrees and education via distance learning and campus colleges. The site features 6,765 accredited online degrees and 13,578 campus-based degree programs. To start your search, visit: **www. directoryofschools.com**.

Of course there are many more sites that can help you find the right online school, you might want to conduct a search on a few of them.

The Application Process

Once you have decided on which schools to apply to, the next step is to fill out the applications. Usually this is a straightforward process, but it can be time consuming. Most applications require more or less the same information, so keep a folder for each school and make copies of everything, including admissions essays. This will prevent you from having to repeat your work for each school. Also, pay attention to admission deadlines. They can vary greatly from school to school.

The admission packets are usually composed of some or all of these elements:

- **The application:** For many schools, the application can be completed online, but if you are using the paper version, be sure to use a typewriter. Handwritten applications look sloppy and can be difficult to read. Be sure to fill out the forms completely and answer all of the questions.

- **The transcripts:** These will need to be sent from your school. It will be easier to send them all at once so that you do not overlook anything. You also want get a copy for yourself, and you should look them over carefully. Mistakes, such as incorrect grades and missing courses, have been known to occur.

To order transcripts you can contact your schools directly; some offer order forms online. Other times, you can write to them with a signed request. There is generally a small fee of around $5 per transcript. You can also order transcripts from The National Student Clearinghouse, described as "the nation's trusted source for post-secondary and secondary student degree, diploma, and enrollment verification." Contact them at **www.studentclearinghouse.org**.

- **Recommendations:** Choose people in authority who know you well, and who you think will not only write a positive essay for you, but will also get it done on time. A great recommendation is not going to do you any good if the admissions office never gets it. Good choices are teachers, administrators, guidance counselors, and ministers. If you have held a job for a while and have done well, talk to your boss about writing one of the letters. Admissions officials are impressed by a good work ethic.

- **The essay:** Be honest. Do not pad your achievements. You want to highlight your accomplishments and the talents that you actually possess. What the admissions office is looking for is whether you are going to be a good fit for their school, so keep in mind why you chose to apply to that school in the first place. If you have done your homework and chosen schools that match your needs, this will not be a problem. Finally, have several people read it and offer suggestions for improvement. Your English teacher or guidance counselor would be a good choice. They can catch mistakes and polish your essay so that you look as good as possible.

- **The interview**: Most colleges do not require an interview because it is not practical, but there is a chance that you are going to find yourself in front of an admissions officer at some point. Dress nicely and be prepared to answer the questions honestly and in a straightforward manner. You should already know why you want to attend that particular school and why you would be an asset for them. Prepare a few personal stories that reveal episodes of your life that taught you an important lesson or were growth experiences for you. If the interviewer questions your grades or SAT score, admit your shortcomings, and discuss how you are working to overcome them.

Wrapping It Up

Once the applications are in the mail, an important step toward college has been completed. Hopefully, the process of choosing a school has helped you find out more about yourself and what you want to do in life. As you wait on the acceptance letters, however, you are not going to have time to rest. The next step is financial aid, which will help you pay for the college of your dreams.

In the meantime, you could be visiting campuses, looking at your budget to see if you can cut costs, and looking at online options as a possibility for at least some of your classes, instead of waiting for the mail carrier to arrive.

3
The Numbers Game

The Free Application for Federal Student Aid (FAFSA) is the most important application you will encounter. Schools, government agencies, and many scholarship committees use the Student Aid Report (SAR) to determine need, which determines how much money you are going to get. This chapter walks you through this process and offers tactics and tips to maximize your benefits. Understanding how financial aid officers and others determine your need is the best way to ensure that you get all that you deserve.

Private colleges may use a different financial aid application called the College Board's CSS/Financial Aid PROFILE application. Some colleges — for example, the University of Pennsylvania — require additional forms that have to be filled out and sent directly to that school. In short, you have to find out for each school that you are applying to exactly what their requirements are for financial aid applications.

You are not going to know the exact amount of financial

aid you are going to receive until April, but you can get a rough estimate now which might help you in planning. Your financial need is the Cost of Attendance (COA), minus your Expected Family Contribution (EFC), which is the amount that you and your family are expected to pay out of pocket for your education. The goal here is to follow strategies to reduce your EFC to the minimum, which will increase the amount of aid you will be eligible to receive. Here is the good news: your EFC does not increase if the COA increases, so if you choose a more expensive school, you are actually eligible for more aid.

Worksheets are available online at **www.finaid.org/ calculators**. These can help you get organized and learn how the process works.

What Is the FAFSA?

The FAFSA is a form that documents important facts about you and your family's financial situation, including income and assets. It is used by college officials to ration aid to the families who need it the most. Essentially, colleges have an alloted amount of money for all of their students, and they dole it out using the FAFSA.

Even if you think that you are not going to be eligible for aid, it is wise to apply anyway. There is no objective way to tell if you are going to be turned down, and the amount you receive can depend on many factors. For example, if your family has multiple children in college, your chances of winning aid increase considerably. Also, as tuition and the other costs of attending college continue to rise, the number of families eligible for aid also increases. So, if you are not eligible for aid your freshman year, rising costs may make you eligible your sophomore, junior, or senior year. The only way you are going to know is to fill out the forms and complete the process.

Families in the upper income brackets, for example over $250,000 a year, can still benefit from the FAFSA. You are not going to get Pell Grants, but you will be eligible for unsubsidized student loans, such as the Stafford and PLUS loans, which might be a good option for you. You will not be eligible for these loans without a FAFSA.

Private scholarships that are based all or in part on your financial needs may also use the FAFSA as the basis for their decisions. For this reason, keep careful records and copies of everything connected with your financial aid application.

You have to do this for every year you attend college, so the more you know about it, the better you will be able to maximize your financial aid opportunities.

Filing Tips

You can start on the FAFSA after January 1 of your senior year, and you do not have to wait until your family's taxes are done before you can complete the job. You can even start the FAFSA preapplication process in November to give you a head start. You can print out the preapplication and fill it in by hand to help you organize the information you will need on the FAFSA.

The FAFSA form is available from many sources. You can get the paper version from your high school counselor's office, the financial aid office at any college, the public library, or by calling 1-800-4-FED-AID (1-800-433-3243). It might be worthwhile to fill out a sample FAFSA form while you are in your sophomore or junior year of high school to familiarize yourself with the form and see how it is going to end up. Of course, you are not going to be able to tell how much aid you might be eligible for, but you can get some idea of how you might be able to reduce your EFC by the time you have to complete the form for real.

An alternative to the paper version is the Web version at **www.fafsa.ed.gov**. This method has several advantages over the paper version. Just like filing taxes online, filing your FAFSA online will get you your SAR a few weeks earlier than if you used the paper version. Also, the Web version has a built-in error-check system. Finally, the Web version makes it easier to file a Renewal FAFSA, which you have to do every year.

The Web version requires that you get a Personal Identification Number (PIN), which is available at **www. pin.ed.gov**. You can also use the PIN as your electronic signature. Since you can use your PIN for all your college years that you are going to be filing a FAFSA, be sure to write it down and keep it with your records.

When you are ready to start, you need to get your financial documents together. You are going to need, at a minimum:

- Your driver's license and social security card

- Your income tax returns for the previous year. If you are married, you will also need your spouse's returns.

- Your parents' income tax returns for the previous year

- Your parents' social security numbers

- Recent bank statements

- Statements relating to stocks, bonds, mutual funds, money market accounts, prepaid tuition plans, Section 529 savings plans, Coverdell Education Savings Accounts, and other investments

- Statements showing nontaxable income such as Veteran's Benefits, Social Security income, or AFDC

- Family-owned business and farm records

Deadlines for filing the FAFSA vary by state, so be sure to check with the financial aid departments of the schools you are applying to. The FAFSA Web site at **www.fafsa.ed.gov** also maintains a list of state deadlines. Most deadlines are around March 1, but the goal should be to complete the form by February 15.

If your family's taxes are not done by then you will have to estimate based on end-of-year pay stubs or some other method. This is likely to happen, because many firms do not have W-2s ready until the end of January, and you may have to wait even longer on 1099s and other documents you need. If you pay someone to prepare and file your taxes, then you might have a further wait, especially if your taxes are complicated and your preparer is buried in work. File the FAFSA anyway. Even if you are self-employed, you should have a close idea of what you made for the year. You can always make corrections later once your taxes have been filed. An alternative is to file your taxes early and then make any corrections with an amended return, but this could add an additional complication to your life. Just make sure you get the FAFSA done.

Filing out the FAFSA is a lot like doing your taxes. If your family has always paid someone to prepare your taxes and never really paid attention to the result, you might have some trouble with the terminology. Follow the instructions and you should be fine. Unless you have really complicated business finances, you should be able to complete the form in a couple of hours.

When you are filling out the forms, be careful to avoid these common mistakes:

- Do not leave any blanks. If the question does not apply to your situation, put 0.

- Include in your untaxed income any Earned Income Credit you received or retirement fund contributions you made.

- Be sure to answer the questions about your parents' education. If you are a first-generation college student, you might qualify for a state grant.

- Always answer "yes" when asked about the different kinds of aid you are interested in, even if you are not. Answering "no" is not going to get more grant money.

- You will be asked a question about which federal income tax form you filed — 1040, 1040A, or 1040EZ. What this question is actually asking is which form you are eligible to file, which can make a difference in the amount of aid you will receive. So put 1040A or

1040EZ, unless you had no choice but file the 1040.

- Do not skip worksheets A, B, and C, which appear at the end of the application.

Double-check everything, and, as always, keep a copy. The first one is the hard one. The Renewal FAFSA, which you will complete in subsequent years, mostly involves putting in any changes to your income and expenses.

What Parents Can Do

There are several strategies for getting the most money you can from the financial aid process. When you file your taxes, you or your tax preparer looks for deductions and strategies to reduce your tax burden, and you should follow the same strategy on the FAFSA. The rules and regulations apply the same way to everybody, so it is definitely within the realm of fairness for you to follow every avenue the law allows to increase the amount of aid you can receive.

A word of caution: do not cheat. The temptation may be great, but the penalties are also great. You could be fined as much as $20,000 and face up to five years in prison. Also, keep in mind that colleges are required to verify the FAFSA applications of at least 30 percent of their students, and many schools verify a much higher percentage. If you are chosen for verification, you will be required to produce the documents that you used to complete the form. The chance of verification is another reason to keep copies of everything.

If you feel that a strategy you are considering might be illegal, or it makes you feel uneasy, feel free to talk it over with a financial aid administrator. They have years of experience at this and have seen it all. Their job is to help you, and they can offer sound advice to help you maximize your eligibility.

There may not be a single strategy that will automatically get you where you want to be. The best thing to do is to test different strategies against your situation and decide which one(s) is going to give you the best result.

The basic idea for maximizing benefits is to reduce income, reduce included assets like savings accounts, and take advantage of the difference between how income and assets of parents and students are computed.

If you and your parents have money in savings accounts, your money should go toward college expenses first. Student assets are counted at a higher percentage than parent's assets, so when your savings have been used up, you will actually be eligible for more aid than if your parents' money was used first.

If your parents are planning to use some of their savings to make a major purchase in the next couple of years, make it now. Putting a down payment on a new car, buying a new refrigerator, remodeling the kitchen, or whatever it is that you are going to need in the near future can actually pay off by reducing your savings assets now, rather than in your junior or senior year of college. Spending money to save money sounds crazy, but remember that this is a numbers game, and you have to use the rules to your advantage if you want to win.

Many people receive an end-of-year bonus in December. You can ask your boss if you can defer it until after January 1.

That will keep it off this year's books and result in a larger aid package. You will have to declare it on the second year's FAFSA, but the college will have planned to set aside the first year's aid for all four years. In other words, you might end up with a larger package for all four years instead of just the first.

Avoid capital gains. If you have property that you are planning to sell, put it off until after the final FAFSA has been filed away during the student's junior year. Selling property turns an asset into income, which is counted at a higher rate and reduces your aid.

Divorced Parents

How divorce is going to affect a student's financial aid opportunities depends on several factors. Divorce can also be ugly, and bitterness can creep into the financial aid process. There are cases where one parent has refused to fill out the FAFSA form. If the marriage is in the process of breaking up at the same time that you are trying to get the aid application together, life can get especially tough.

Divorce and separation can lead to a variety of complicated family relationships, but the financial aid process focuses on you and whose house you are living in. "Custodial parent" is the key concept for aid purposes, and it means the parent that you live with for more than half of the year. It makes no difference who has legal custody or who is responsible for paying child support.

For example, if Jimmy's parents divorced two years ago, and he lives with his father, the Dad is the custodial parent and they have a family of two persons. Only Dad's income and assets will be considered, although Mom may have to file a FAFSA. If Dad remarries, even if it is the day he fills out the FAFSA form, there is now a family of three and the both Dad and his new wife's income and assets will have to be included on the FAFSA, along with any children the new wife brings to the family. And when those children need financial aid, their new stepfather's income and assets will be considered along with their mom's assets.

This scenario is straightforward, but things can get confusing very quickly. Parents are accustomed to thinking of the children who live with them in terms of tax exemptions, which are based not only on where the child lives, but also on who provides their support, or even who was granted the exemption by court order. Financial aid does not work that way. If a stepchild lives in your house, but receives more than 50 percent of his support from an ex-spouse, you cannot claim that child as a tax exemption, but he or she is part of your household for financial aid purposes. That child's biological parent would have to claim any child support received as untaxed income. What counts is where the child physically spends most of his or her time.

Another difference between financial aid rules and IRS rules is that a child can be a tax exemption for only one person, but can be counted as part of more than one household for financial aid purposes. Let us say that Jack and Jill have a son named William. Jack and Jill get divorced, and as part of the agreement William lives with Jill but Jack provides more than 50 percent of his support. Jack remarries, and his new wife has a daughter the same age as William and they are both ready for college. Jack gets to claim his new daughter, as well as his son, for whom he is providing support, as part of his household. His new daughter will get more financial aid because Jack will have two children in college. When William's mother fills out his FAFSA, she also gets to claim William as part of her household. Even though she does not provide more than 50 percent of his support, she is the custodial parent. Therefore, William is counted as being in two households for aid purposes.

The PROFILE

Many private schools require the PROFILE form as a supplement to the FAFSA. Unlike the FAFSA, you have to register for the PROFILE form on the College Board's Web site (**www.collegeboard.com**) and pay a $5 registration fee, as well as an $18 processing fee for every school that you want to send the completed form to. You need to be sure which schools you want to apply to, and whether they require this form, to save yourself some headaches.

The PROFILE covers much of the same ground as the FAFSA, but the College Board also maintains a database of questions that are used by individual schools to go gather more detail than the FAFSA. For example, PROFILE filers have to produce three years of income information instead of one, and also have to provide additional information about home ownership. On the positive side, the PROFILE can allow for more expenses than the FAFSA form.

When you register and choose the schools that will receive the form, the Web site automatically brings up these school-specific questions for you and takes care of delivering the answers to the right school.

If you are filing the FAFSA, the PROFILE, and perhaps

additional school-specific forms, you need to make sure that you have been consistent across the forms.

The Student Aid Report (SAR)

Now that you have sent in all the forms (after making copies of everything) it is time to relax and wait for a few weeks. It takes three to four weeks to get your SAR via either regular mail or e-mail, depending on which option you chose. In either case, this is an important document and you should make sure that you keep a copy along with all of the other forms you have accumulated to this point.

Check the SAR to make sure that the numbers are accurate and that it has been sent to the correct schools. If you have decided to apply at additional schools, contact the financial aid office at those schools for further instructions. If the schools want you to send them your original copy, be sure to order additional copies for yourself.

The SAR will give you two important pieces of information. The first is whether you are eligible for the Pell Grant, which is free money the government gives to low-income students.

The second piece of information the SAR gives you is your Expected Family Contribution (EFC). This is the SAT score of financial aid. Except that in this case, the lower the number, the more aid you are going to get.

If your EFC is way out of line with what you can actually pay, you can ask the financial aid office for a professional judgment, which is a review of your EFC owing to special circumstances. If you have unusually high medical bills, for example, your financial aid officer may reduce your EFC.

An important consideration when going this route is to do it before you actually commit to the school. The financial aid officer may be more cooperative if more aid will ensure that you attend that school.

Be aware, however, that a professional judgment in your favor is not necessarily going to result in more free money. More likely, your offer of loans is going to increase.

The Offers

The college's financial aid offer usually arrives along with an acceptance letter. The offer will most likely contain a combination of several components: grants, loans, and work-study.

The financial aid officer who completes your package goes about it in this manner. First, he or she will calculate the cost of attendance, taking into consideration whether you are a residential or commuter student. Your EFC is subtracted from this figure, along with any federal or state grants. Scholarships and other outside funding are also subtracted.

That usually leaves some costs, referred to as the remaining financial need (RFN). This need is met with federal loans and federal work-study, which in financial aid terms is referred to as self-help, because it is a contribution over and above the EFC. Colleges try to level out the self-help amounts, because they have the most direct impact on families.

When financial aid officers are figuring all of these components for an individual student, they look at eligibility, need, and merit. Eligibility for loans and grants is usually straightforward. Either you meet the criteria or you do not. Need can be more subjective. Colleges have a certain amount of grant money available, and they can choose to give the bulk of it to the more unfortunate students, or they could distribute it among most of the student population. This choice could have a big impact on whether you receive loans or grants, and it is why aid offers can vary greatly from school to school.

Merit aid is subjective and reflects the needs and values of the school. The school controls this money, so they can decide if they want to use it to attract students with special abilities in athletics, music, academics, or drama. Some schools have dropped merit aid entirely, and give out money based solely on need. The more selective the school, the less likely they are to hand out merit aid, because they have less need to attract talented students.

Financial aid officers take care to address each individual student's needs with all of this in mind. But since schools operate with different goals and values in mind, offers from different schools will vary even though they are working with the same basic raw material.

Comparing Offers

Make a chart that lists the amounts of aid you are going to receive, then make another chart that compares loan amounts and your own contributions. For instance, it sounds great if a school offers you $20,000 in aid for the year, but it might not be a good deal if you are left with $10,000 in loans to repay and $6,000 to pay out of pocket. Similarly, a school that offers you only $12,000 in aid but leaves you with a smaller amount of loans and money you have to pay yourself is a better deal. What you need to do is make a chart that lists the amounts of aid you are going to receive, then make another chart that compares loan amounts and your own contributions. These are the important numbers at this point.

It should be easy to see which school is the best bargain for you, but it might not be the school you choose to attend. You might decide that it is worth the extra cost to attend a more prestigious school, or you may simply be willing to pay more to attend a school that you like better. The choice is ultimately up to you.

Before you sign on the dotted line, there is one final step. As we have seen, the financial aid offer is partly the result of a subjective process. That means there is some room for negotiation. Financial aid officers can exercise what is called "professional judgment" to increase, or in some cases ,radically improve offers of aid. Do not assume, however, that the negotiations are going to work. If the financial aid package from the school you want to attend has made it easily affordable for you, then it is probably a great deal already and you are not going to get any more. The financial aid office knows what other students are getting, and is not going to listen long to whining.

If the school you want to attend really has provided an unworkable package, or if you have received radically different packages from similar schools and the school you want is on the bottom side, then it is worth it to negotiate. It is especially worthwhile if the school really wants you because of your high SAT and/or ACT scores, grade point average, or special talents. They are going to be less likely to budge if you barely made it in, but they do want to be fair.

Parents: do not go into a professional judgment interview and complain about your high credit card debt, the payments on your new boat, or the gambling debts that have left you strapped. There are problems that you created, and financial aid officers who probably do not make as much as you do are not going to have much sympathy.

Legitimate circumstances that are not covered by the FAFSA can leave you with an unrealistic aid package. Unusual capital gains, a recent bankruptcy, termination of a child support agreement, unusually high medical expenses, or a drop in income are legitimate reasons to ask for a review of your case.

Have a plan ready. If you or your parents are basing your argument on a peculiar financial situation, such as support of an elderly relative or unusually high unreimbursed business expenses, be prepared to document your case. Similarly, if your argument in based on radically different aid packages from similar schools, be prepared to show them the aid letters. They will probably ask to see them anyway. If there has been a drastic change in your life since you filed the aid forms — divorce, job loss — let the financial aid office know about it. If you make a good case and the school wants you, they will make a better offer that could save you thousands of dollars. At this point, they really do not have a lot of money left to throw your way, so even if the upgrade is small, walk away happy. Even if things are not going your way, the worst thing they can do is say no, and they cannot take back an offer they have already made. So, you have nothing to lose.

When you are ready to accept, you have one decision left to make. The financial aid package is comprised of several components, and you have the option of rejecting one or all of these. You may, for instance, want to reject a work-study offer or even a loan offer if you have a better way of making up the difference. Be aware, however, that rejecting any kind of aid may lessen the amount that you receive in coming years, when you might really need it. And keep in mind that you can usually walk away from a work-study program at any time if it does not work out for you. Check out your school's regulations on this before you try it.

Some Good News

After all of this detail about how much college is going to cost you, it is time for a little good news. Paying for college offers some significant tax benefits. The rules tend to change, so you might want to consult a tax advisor.

The Hope tax credit provides a $1,500 tax credit for the first two years of out-of-pocket tuition and fee expenses per student. For parents with more than one student in school, this can be a major break. The key words here are out-of-pocket. Also, there are income limits.

The Lifetime Learning Tax Credit kicks in after your Hope eligibility is gone. This credit is for 20 percent of your qualified tuition expenses, no matter who they are for, up to a limit of $2,000. The best part is that this credit is good indefinitely, but it does have the same income limits as the Hope Scholarship.

After graduation, student loan interest that you have paid during the year is an above-the-line income, which means that it reduces your adjusted gross income. There are income limitations, so if your parents are not going to get this benefit, you might want to be sure that any student loans are in your name, so you can claim the deduction. The regulations state that only the person legally obligated to repay the loan can take the deduction, regardless of who is actually making the payments. Only the person who signed the bottom line is going to get the tax benefits.

Depending on your income and your parents' income, these tax benefits can reduce your actual expenditures to zero. Keep in mind, though, that these tax goodies tend to change frequently, so keep an eye out at tax time for any changes.

Wrapping It Up

The financial aid process can be the most daunting task of preparing for college. It is complicated and confusing at times, and frustrating at others. But it must be done, and the payoff makes it worth all of the work. Like everything else connected with college, do your research and study hard. You can make the financial aid process work for you, and you can afford college. With the right tools and some hard work, your application and aid letters will deliver the goods right to your door.

The FAFSA, although important, is only a part of the process of getting money for college. In the next chapters, you will discover how scholarships, grants, and work opportunities offer excellent ways of paying for college. You can combine these with your financial aid package, or add to it. Unbelievably, we are only getting started.

4

Grants

efore we consider loan money that you can borrow and pay back, let us explore money you do not have to pay back: grants. Grants are a great way to cut the costs of college, and grant money does not have to be returned. While scholarships are generally based on performance, grants are often (but not always), based on need. Grants can range from $100 to covering full tuition costs at a four-year college or university. They can be a great supplement to your financing for college, as it is that much less that you have to borrow or get from another source. Plus, once you finish college, it will be that much less you have to pay back. After all, loan payments can be a hefty check to write out every month for years on end, even with the low-interest loans students have access to. A monthly payment for a student loan can easily reach the $200 to $500 per month range, so it is in your best interest to take advantage of all the free money to which you are entitled. Most students end up wishing they had borrowed less, as the payments can be very hard to manage. Although loans make it possible for many to attend school, loans are still debt that has to be paid back. Your goal should be to keep your debt down to a minimum, and one way to do it is to take advantage of grants. Apply for as many as you can.

So how do you find out about grants? A good place to start is with the financial aid office of the college that you will be attending. The financial aid office is familiar with both state and federal grants that are available to students. There are also Web sites that can help you track down grants that may be available from private sources, which we will explore shortly. Private sources may be companies that are using grants for college as public relations tools (while utilizing the possible tax deduction), or they may be offered by a private individual that is trying to assist certain kinds of students with certain kinds of needs. For instance, the grant may be designed for American Indian students who are planning to use their studies to help on a reservation. They may be specific, such as a grant designed for single mothers studying dentistry, or they may be broad such as art students who are working on their BFA degree at a specific art college.

If you look hard enough, you will certainly find a grant for which you are qualified to apply. A great site you can try is **www.fastweb.com**. This is a popular site that many college financial aid offices recommend as a supplemental source to find and apply for private grants, along with other funding. According to FastWeb, they are "recommended by over 15,500 high schools and 3,500 colleges." FastWeb users answer a detailed questionnaire, and the data then generates possibilities for scholarships, grants, internships, and more, all based on your input. This saves you time and effort, as the information given to you is for suitable possibilities, meaning money for which you are qualified to apply. However, you can search the whole database if you desire.

Although many of the grants that are available are given out according to financial need, some grants are merit based, while others are designed to promote a particular field of study or to encourage students to attend private schools. For instance, you may find a grant that is specifically designed for those who are studying art at a private college, or you may find a grant designed for those who plan on working in human services. You may find grants that require a high GPA for a particular field of study, such as math or science. There are plenty of private grants out there, and you may be qualified for more than one grant. Private grants can be used in addition to government grants, both of which we will go over shortly in more detail.

One thing to consider about a grant, whether it is a private or a government grant, is that they are created to help you defray the costs of college. They are not designed to be used for a vacation to Bermuda, a new stereo system for your dorm room, a down payment on a new vehicle, or new clothing for your wardrobe. They are specifically designed to be used for tuition, books, and other school supplies. Many grants pay the funds to the school directly, so the money never reaches your hands.

As with all your financial planning for college, be sure to apply for grant money early. Many grant funds are limited. Every deadline differs, but it is generally a good idea to get all of your financial applications in by February 15.

Federal Grants

Federal grants are, by definition, an award of financial assistance from a federal agency. As presented in Chapter 3, one of the fist steps you will want to take when applying for a federal grant is to fill out the Free Application for Federal Student Aid, or FAFSA form. Remember, you can find the form at high schools and college financial aid offices, at **www.fafsa.ed.gov**, or by calling the Federal Student Aid, an office of the U.S. Department of Education, at 1-800-4-FED-AID (1-800-433-3243). Again, make sure you file the form as early as possible, as some grants have limited funds for the year.

Pell Grants

The name "Pell Grant" is in honor of Senator Claiborne Pell from Rhode Island. He was a long-time advocate of federal funding for higher education, thus it seemed appropriate to name a grant after him. Pell Grants provide more than 90 percent of all federal grant money (veterans' benefits excluded). They are awarded to undergraduates who have not received a bachelor's degree. Pell Grants are based on the financial needs of the applicant, taking into consideration the size of the student's household, the amount of their yearly income, and the cost of tuition at the school the student has chosen. This information is based on what you submit in the Free Application for Federal Student Aid (FAFSA), as described in Chapter 3. Since 2002, the maximum amount of a Pell Grant per award year has remained at $4,050, although the maximum amount is set every year depending on the funding. The amount of the grant is determined by the student's cost of attending school, and whether the student will be a full-time or part-time student. A student's eligibility is determined by the Expected Family Contribution (EFC), the amount that you and your family are expected to pay out of pocket for your education. To qualify for the Pell Grant, you need to have an EFC of $3,850 or less. While it is possible to receive a Pell Grant if your family's household income is $50,000 or more, most recipients' household income is under $20,000. The lower the EFC, the more likely you will be to receive the grant. You may receive the Pell Grant for every year that you work toward your education, as there is no limit on the number of times you receive it. However, you may only receive one Pell Grant per year.

Some of the eligibility requirements to receive a Pell Grant include:

- You must demonstrate a financial need by submitting a Free Application for Federal Student Aid (FAFSA).

- You must be a U.S citizen or an eligible noncitizen.

- You must have a high school diploma or a GED.

- You must not have defaulted on any student loans.

- You must have a valid Social Security Number.

- You must be enrolled in an eligible postsecondary school.

- You must be working toward a first undergraduate degree or teaching credential.

- Male applicants must have registered for the Selective Service, if they are between the ages of 18 and 25.

- Satisfactory academic progress must be maintained.

- You must certify that the funds will be used only for educational purposes.

The following people are ineligible to receive a Pell Grant:

- Those who owe a refund on a grant made by a federal student aid program under Title IV of the Higher Education Act.

- Those who default on a Title IV loan.

- Those who are incarcerated.

- Those who have been convicted of possessing or selling illegal drugs.

Things to keep in mind with a Pell Grant are that not every school participates in the federal grant program, some degree programs are ineligible, you may receive only one Pell Grant in an award year, and you may not receive Pell Grant funds from more than one school at a time. You may also receive a Pell Grant for every academic year until you receive a bachelor's degree, and the grant can be transferred to another school if you change schools within an aid year. Always ask your college's financial aid office about a Pell Grant, even if you think you may not be eligible.

There are times when special circumstances may come into play when considering the amount that you will receive.

The special circumstance may include something like a student who incurred major medical expenses that are not covered by insurance policies. Also, if you have disability-related expenses, such as wheelchairs, interpreters, and personal attendants, they can used to help enhance your award amount. Your school's financial aid office can assist with making a case for special circumstances.

The Pell Grant has requirements regarding residency, starting with the fact you must be able to live and attend school legally in the United States as a U.S. citizen, a U.S. national, or an eligible noncitizen.

Eligible noncitizens would include those who are:

- U.S. permanent residents (Alien Registration Card or I-551)

- Conditional permanent residents (I-551C Card)

- Refugees, asylum grantees, or parolees

- Cuban-Haitian entrants with Arrival Departure Records (I-94) from the Immigration and Naturalization Service (INS).

If you are collecting Social Security (SSI), you may still receive the Pell Grant without jeopardizing your SSI eligibility. Unlike other money you might receive, grants are not considered income or assets if they are used for school purposes, such as tuition, fees, or other education expenses. The same goes if you are receiving Social Security Disability Insurance (SSDI.) You may still receive the Pell Grant while collecting SSDI.

If you are collecting Social Security due to a disability, you might want to consider a Plan for Achieving Self-Support (PASS). A PASS will allow you to set aside otherwise countable income and/or resources for a specific period in order to achieve a work goal. According to the Social Security Administration, "Under SSI rules, any income that you have may reduce your SSI payment. But, if you have an approved plan, you can use that income to pay for the items you need to reach your work goal." A PASS can be used for tuition, books, or other supplies needed to attend school. You must have the PASS plan approved first. You can find out more by calling the Social Security Administration at 1-800-772-1213, or by visiting **www.ssa.gov**.

Academic Competitiveness Grant and National SMART Grants

According to the U.S. Department of Education, two new grants are available (as of 2006-2007) to those that are studying topics in math, science, technology, engineering, and critical foreign languages: The Academic Competitiveness Grant (ACG) and National Science and Mathematics Access to Retain Talent (National SMART Grant) Programs. These are performance-based and are awarded to those who have demonstrated a financial need.

If you are in your first and second academic year of college, you may be eligible for the Academic Competitiveness Grant and receive up to $750 for the first year of study and up to $1,300 for the second year. During your third and fourth academic years, you may be eligible for a National SMART

Grant and receive up to $4,000 for each year of study.

Requirements for Academic Competitiveness Grant and National SMART Grants are, for each year of study:

- You must be a U.S. citizen.

- You must be attending school full-time in a four-year degree-granting institution.

- You must be eligible to receive a Pell Grant.

- You must meet other eligibility requirements related to — depending on your year in school — completing a rigorous high school curriculum; majoring in mathematics, science, or selected foreign languages; and maintaining a required minimum grade point average (GPA).

Keep in mind that only certain learning institutions participate in the program. If you are eligible to receive either grant, the funds may go directly to your student account at the school, or the funds may be paid directly to you. Or it may be a combination of both — some funds go in your school account and the rest are given to you. For more information, ask your financial aid office at your high school or college, or visit the U.S. Department of Education at: **www.studentaid. ed.gov** or call the Federal Student Aid Information Center (FSAIC) 1-800-4-FED-AID (1-800-433-3243).

Supplemental Educational Opportunity Grants

Other federal grants that are need-based are the Federal

Supplemental Education Opportunity Grants (SEOG). SEOG grants range from $100 to $4,000, and are distributed at least once per term (semester, trimester, or quarter), at least twice per academic year.

The grants are designed for undergraduates, or vocational students, who are enrolled in school at least half-time, and are pursuing their first bachelor's degree. Students who are already receiving a Pell Grant are given priority to receive a SEOG. Determination is made by Expected Family Contribution (EFC) score, which was determined on their financial aid application, and they are awarded to the less fortunate students first. But unlike a Pell Grant, there is a possibility that a student awarded a SEOG will not receive the money. Colleges receive a limited amount of funding for the program each year; therefore, they can only give the grant to so many students per year. Some schools do not participate in the program. Check with your school's financial aid office for more details about the SEOG.

Leveraging Educational Assistance Partnership (LEAP)

The Leveraging Educational Assistance Partnership is also known as the "LEAP Program." Instead of providing grants directly to students, the program provides grants to states in order to help them provide their own need-based grants and community service work-study assistance. The states each apply for this federal program, and they administer the program under a single state agency. The agency must follow certain criteria. Both undergraduate and graduate students, who must demonstrate a large financial need, may apply for the program in the state that they are residents. Some of the eligibility requirements for the program are:

- You must demonstrate financial need.

- You must be eligible to receive the Pell Grant.

- You must be a U.S. citizen, or an eligible noncitizen.

- You must not have defaulted on any student loans.

- Male applicants must have registered for the Selective Service.

- Satisfactory academic progress must be maintained.

Other stipulations may be required. Check with your state's human services department, or ask your school's financial aid office to help point you in the right direction.

In addition to the LEAP Program, there is the SLEAP Program, which is available to states that participate in the LEAP program. According to the U.S. Department of Education, "The SLEAP Program assists states in providing student aid programs for eligible students pursuing their postsecondary education and who have substantial financial need. The student aid programs can be in the form of supplemental grants, supplemental community service work-study employment, or merit and academic achievement or critical career scholarships." Both undergraduate and graduate students with financial needs may apply to their residential state.

For more information, visit **www.ed.gov**, call the Federal Student Aid Information Center 800-433-3243 or 800-4FED-AID, or ask your school's financial aid office.

Federal Agency Grants

Federal agency grants are grants that come from places like the National Endowment for the Arts, an independent federal agency. Federal agency grants are awarded for reasons other than education, such as projects and research. Every federal agency that offers grants has its own set of eligibility requirements, all depending on the type of grant and the agency itself. One of the best resources to check for federal agency grants is **www.grants.gov**. There are 26 federal grant-making agencies available through the site that you can link to and apply for grants with. There are 1,000 Federal agency grants available, with approximately $400 billion in annual awards, some of which are for educational purposes or can be used to help fund education. Grants are designed for everyone from small businesses, to organizations, to individuals, all of which you can easily research on the site. According to Grants.gov, the federal agencies that provide grants include:

- **Agency for International Development:** An independent federal government agency that provides economic and humanitarian assistance in more than 100 countries.

- **Corporation for National and Community Service:** The nation's largest grant-maker supporting service and volunteering.

- **Department of Agriculture:** Serves all Americans through antihunger efforts, stewardship of nearly 200 million acres of national forest and rangelands, and through product safety and conservation efforts.

- **Department of Commerce:** Fosters and promotes the nation's economic development and technological advancement through vigilance in international trade policy, domestic business policy and growth, and promoting economic progress at all levels.

- **Department of Defense:** Provides the military forces needed to deter war and protect the security of the United States, including peacekeeping, war-fighting efforts, evacuation, and humanitarian causes.

- **Department of Education:** Ensures equal access to education and promotes educational excellence through coordination, management, and accountability in federal education programs.

- **Department of Energy:** Advances national, economic, and energy security in the U.S.; promotes scientific and technological innovation in support of that goal; and ensures environmental cleanup of the national nuclear weapons complex.

- **Department of Health and Human Services:** The federal government's principal agency for protecting the health of all Americans and providing essential human services, especially to those who are least able to help themselves.

- **Department of Homeland Security:** Has three

primary missions: Prevent terrorist attacks within the United States, reduce America's vulnerability to terrorism, and minimize the damage from potential attacks and natural disasters.

- **Department of Housing and Urban Development:** Their mission is to increase homeownership, support community development, and increase access to affordable housing free from discrimination.

- **Department of the Interior:** Protects and provides access to the Nation's natural and cultural heritage, including responsibilities to Indian tribes and island communities.

- **Department of Justice:** Enforces the law and defends the interest of the United States, ensuring public safety against threats foreign and domestic; provides federal leadership in preventing and controlling crime; seeks just punishment for those guilty of unlawful pursuits; and ensures fair and impartial administration of justice for all Americans.

- **Department of Labor:** Fosters and promotes the welfare of job seekers, wage earners, and retirees by improving their working conditions, advancing their opportunities, protecting their retirement and health benefits, and generally protecting worker rights and monitoring national economic measures.

- **Department of State:** Strives to create a more secure, democratic, and prosperous world for the benefit of the American people and the international community.

- **Department of Transportation:** Their mission is to ensure fast, safe, efficient, accessible, and convenient transportation that meets vital national interests and enhances the quality of life of the American people, today and into the future.

- **Department of the Treasury:** A steward of United States economic and financial systems, they promote conditions for prosperity and stability in the U.S., and encourage prosperity and stability in the rest of the world.

- **Department of Veterans Affairs:** Strives for excellence in patient care and veteran's benefits for its constituents through high quality, prompt, and seamless service to United States veterans.

- **Environmental Protection Agency**: Their mission is to protect human health and the environment.

- **Institute of Museum and Library Services:** The primary source of federal support for the nation's 122,000 libraries and 17,500 museums.

- **National Aeronautics and Space Administration:** Serves as the nation's forefront of such exploration and continues to pioneer in aeronautics, exploration systems, science, and space operations.

- **National Archives and Records Administration:** Enables people to inspect the record of what the federal government has done, enables officials and agencies to review their actions, and helps citizens hold them accountable.

- **National Endowment for the Arts:** A public agency dedicated to supporting excellence in the arts; bringing the arts to all Americans and providing leadership in arts education.

- **National Endowment for the Humanities:** An independent grant-making agency of the United States government dedicated to supporting research, education, preservation, and public programs in the humanities.

- **National Science Foundation:** An independent federal agency created to promote the progress of science, to advance the national health, prosperity, and welfare, and to secure the national defense.

- **Small Business Administration:** Maintains and strengthens the nation's economy by aiding, counseling, assisting, and protecting the interests of small businesses and by helping families and businesses recover from national disasters.

- **Social Security Administration:** Advances the economic security of the nation's people through compassionate and vigilant leadership in shaping and managing America's Social Security programs.

State Grants

Most states have grant programs to help with college, however, like many grants they are often need-based. Still, some state grants are designed to assist with certain degree programs, or are merit-based. Keep in mind that some states have signed reciprocity agreements with other states to offer need-based grant programs to out-of-state undergraduates; it is something to consider if you are a resident in a state other than where you are attending college. Also, remember that the yearly budget for grants can change. One year there may be more funds allocated for the grants, meaning more students will receive the grant money, or that the money each student will receive will vary. Generally, the first step is to complete your FAFSA, as presented in Chapter 3.

Just to give you an idea what state grants are available, let us take a look at a few.

Alabama residents can apply for the Alabama Student Assistance Program; a state/federal aid program designed for undergraduate students. Awards range from $300 to $2,500 per year. For more information, call the Alabama Commission of Higher Education at (334) 242-1998, visit **www.ache.state.al.us**, or check with your school's financial aid office.

Cal Grants are offered through the California Student Aid Commission; they are all designed to help students that are pursuing an undergraduate associate's degree, bachelor's degree, or an occupational training program at any qualifying California college, university, or career or technical school. The grants assist low- to middle-income students, those who are attending private or public college, and those who are pursuing vocational or career training. With a Cal Grant, you can receive up to $9,700 a year to help pay for college expenses. Each grant has certain requirements that must be met, such as maintaining a certain GPA. To find out more about Cal Grants, visit **www. calgrants.org**, or the California Student Aid Commission at **www.csac.ca.gov**, or call 888-CA GRANT (224-7268), or ask your financial aid office more information.

Qualified Colorado residents can take advantage of the Colorado National Guard Tuition Assistance Program and get up to 100 percent of tuition costs paid at state-supported institutions. For more information, contact a National Guard recruiter or the state tuition assistance office at (303) 677-8913. Or call the Colorado Department of Education at 303-866-2723, or visit **http://highered. colorado.gov.**

In Florida, residents can apply for the Florida Bright Futures Scholarship Program, a program that establishes three lottery-funded scholarships to reward high school graduates for academic achievement. Or they can apply for other funds, such as the José Martí Scholarship Challenge Grant Fund and receive $2,000 per year. This need-based merit award is designed for eligible students of Hispanic origin who will attend Florida public or eligible private institutions, and who are enrolled in a minimum of 12 credit hours for undergraduate study or 9 credit hours for graduate study. Students must apply during their senior year of high school. For more information, contact the Florida Department of Education's Office of Student Financial Assistance at 888-827-2004, or visit **www.floridastudentfinancialaid.org**, or check with your school's financial aid office.

Georgia residents can apply for the Georgia Tuition Equalization Grant Program that was designed to assist undergraduate students with attending eligible private colleges in Georgia. The amount of the award is $333 per quarter or $500 per semester for up to four quarters or three semesters per year. For more information, visit the Georgia Student Finance Commission at **http://gacollege411. org**, or e-mail **support@GAcollege411.org**.

Illinois offers a "Grant Program for Dependents of Police or Fire Officers" for those who are working on undergraduate and graduate degrees at approved Illinois colleges. According to State of Illinois' site **www.collegezone.com**, "If you are the spouse or child of an Illinois police or fire officer who was killed or became at least 90 percent disabled in the line of duty, you may be eligible for the Grant Program for Dependents of Police or Fire Officers." If eligible, you may receive the equivalent amount of eight semesters or 12 quarters of assistance. Find out more at **www.collegezone.com**, Call the Illinois Student Assistance Commission at 800-899-ISAC (4722), or check your school's financial aid office.

In Maryland, doctoral students can apply for the Southern Regional Education Board (SREB) Doctoral Scholars Program. According to the Maryland Higher Education Commission "[The Program] is designed to increase the number of minority faculty in the 16-state SREB region by encouraging ethnic minorities to pursue doctoral degrees and become college-level teachers." The Doctoral Scholars Program Award is quite generous as it offers five years of support, starting with a waiver of tuition and fees during the first three years, and in the final two years the award is determined on an individual basis. For application information visit the SREB Web site at **www.sreb.org**. For more information about the Southern Regional Education

Board (SREB) Doctoral Scholars Program, contact the Maryland Higher Education Commission at (410) 260-4500, or 800-974-0203, or visit **www.mhec.state.md.us**.

New York residents can take advantage of the Tuition Assistance Program (TAP). It is New York's largest grant program, and it is based on income, or your family's New York State net taxable income. If you are eligible for a TAP grant you can receive up to $5,000 at an approved school. Part-time students are eligible for a part-time TAP. You can find out more and apply for TAP at the New York State Higher Education Services Corporation Web site, **www. hesc.com**, or call (888) NYSHESC, or ask your financial aid office more information.

In North Dakota, residents can take advantage of the North Dakota State Grant. Awards are designed for those who are earning their undergraduate degree and who attend North Dakota's public, private (not-for-profit), and tribal colleges. The awards range from $600 to $1,000 for an academic year. For more information call the North Dakota University System at 701-328-2960, visit **www.ndus.edu**, or check with your school's financial aid office.

North Carolina residents can take advantage of several grant opportunities, including the NC Community College Grant & Loan Program, which is designed for students who are enrolled at North Carolina community colleges. According to the College Foundation of North Carolina, "Eligibility is determined based on the same criteria as the Federal Pell Grant; students not eligible for the Federal Pell Grant may be considered for the grant based on their estimated family contribution as determined on the Student Aid

Report. Students who have earned the baccalaureate (4 year) college degree are ineligible."

The amount of the grant varies according to information that is generated from the Pell Grant application. For more information, call the College Foundation of North Carolina at 888-234-6400 (toll free), visit **www.cfnc.org**, or check with your school's financial aid office.

In Ohio, residents can take advantage of the Ohio College Opportunity Grant (OCOG); a need-based tuition assistance for low- to moderate-income families. First-time freshmen enrolled as full-time, three-quarters time, half-time, or one-quarter-time may be eligible to receive awards that range according to the type of school they are attending. Public: $2,496, private: $4,992, and proprietary: $3,996. For more information, contact the Ohio Board of Regents at 888-833-1133, visit **www.regents.ohio.gov/sgs/ocog**, or check with your school's financial aid office.

Rhode Island residents who qualify can receive the Rhode Island State Grant Program. The program was designed to assist families whose resources are not sufficient to meet the costs of higher education, and the award amount ranges from $250 to $1400 depending on the financial needs of the applicant. Awards can be used at eligible schools in Rhode Island and all over the United States, Canada, and Mexico. They can be renewed every year for up to three years (four years if a student is enrolled in an eligible five-year program of study), and satisfactory progress must be maintained. For more information, contact the Rhode Island Higher Education Assistance Authority at 401-736-1100, or 800-922-9855, visit

www.riheaa.org/borrowers/grants, or check with your school's financial aid office.

If you are a Texas resident who has demonstrated a financial need, you can take advantage of the Tuition Equalization Grant Program (TEG) and receive up to $3,331 per school year. Students who have demonstrated an exceptional financial need may receive up to $4,966 in a given year. To find out more, ask your school's financial aid office, visit College for Texans at **www.collegefortexans.com**, call the Texas Higher Education Coordinating Board's Division of Student Services at 800-242-3062 (outside the Austin area) or at 512-427-6340 (in the Austin area), or check with your school's financial aid office.

Utah offers the Utah Centennial Opportunity Program for Education (UCOPE) Grant for qualified undergraduate residents who are attending schools in Utah. UCOPE grants are funded by the state, and the maximum grant award is $500 per school year, but not all Utah schools offer UCOPE grants. For more information, call the Utah Higher Education Assistance Authority at 800-418-2551, visit **www.uheaa. org**, or check with your school's financial aid office.

Vermont residents enrolled in an undergraduate degree or certificate program who will be attending college full-time, and who do not already have a bachelor's degree, are eligible to apply for a Vermont Incentive Grant. Residents attending the University of Vermont College of Medicine or enrolled in a Doctor of Veterinary medicine program are also eligible to apply. The awards are based on financial need, and they range from $500 to $10,600 per year. They can be used at schools either within Vermont or out of state.

Vermont Part-Time Grants are also available to those who are enrolled in an undergraduate degree or certificate program and who will be attending less than full-time. The grants are based on financial need. Students must be taking fewer than 12 credits per semester and not have already received a bachelor's degree. The amount of each award varies, depending on credit hours. For more information, call Vermont Student Assistance at 800-882-4166 or 802-654-3750, or visit **www.vsac.org**. Or check with your school's financial aid office.

Washington State also offers its residents a state grant program, the Educational Opportunity Grant (EOG). The program is designed for financially needy Washington residents who are working toward a bachelor's degree at an eligible four-year college. Students must have already earned an associate of arts or sciences degree or achieved junior class standing. The grants are $2,500 per academic year, and they can be renewed for one additional academic year. Certain eligibility requirements apply. To find out more, contact the Washington Higher Education Coordinating Board at **www.hecb.wa.gov**, call 360-596-4803, or check with your school's financial aid office.

Wisconsin has several grant programs available to qualified resident students, including the Indian Student Assistance Grant. This grant was designed for undergraduate or graduate students who are at least 25 percent Native American and are enrolled in degree or certificate programs at the University of Wisconsin, Wisconsin Technical College, independent colleges and universities, tribal colleges, or proprietary institutions based in Wisconsin. The grant is based on financial need, it ranges from $250 to $1,100, and it has a limit of ten semesters of eligibility. Students must be enrolled at least part-time (including less than half-time). Minority students (African American, American Indian, Hispanic, or Southeast Asian from Laos, Cambodia, or Vietnam) may apply for the Minority Undergraduate Retention Grant. Grants are based on financial need with a maximum grant of $2,500 per year for up to eight semesters or twelve quarters. For more information, contact the State of Wisconsin Higher Educational Aids Board at 608-267-2206, visit **www.heab.state.wi.us**, or check with your school's financial aid office.

As you can see, many states offer a wide range of grants designed for assistance with higher education. This list was created to show examples of what is available, and it is by no means all-inclusive. For more information about your state's grants, inquire with your state's Department of Education or ask your college financial aid office. The Online Education Database, **www.oedb.org**, also has a search engine for state grants, as well as categories to find grants in everything from minority college grants, to athletic college grants, and grants for women, Native Americans, law school grants, nursing college grants, study-abroad grants, and more. They have 102 accredited colleges and 1,235 programs in their database. The amount of grants available varies state by state.

A Few More Ways to Save on Education

Employee/Dependent of Employee Discounts

Do not forget to ask about Employee/Dependent of

Employee Discounts. For instance, at Mount Carmel College of Nursing in Columbus, Ohio, you can receive a college discount if you are a Mount Carmel employee or the dependent of a Mount Carmel employee. According to the College, "Full-time employees who have completed six months of service are eligible for discounted tuition, as are dependent children (including adopted children and stepchildren) whose parents have completed one year of full-time employment with Mount Carmel." For more information, call 614-234-5800 or 800-556-6942, or visit **www.mccn.edu**.

United States Veterans Programs

If you are a United States veteran, you may be eligible to receive educational benefits from a variety of programs:

- IHL (Institutes of Higher Learning)

- NCD (Non-College Degree Programs)

- On-the-Job & Apprenticeship Training

- Flight Training

- Independent Training, Distance Learning, and Internet Training

- Correspondence Training

- National Testing Program

- Licensing and Certification

- Entrepreneurship Training

- Work-Study Program

- Co-op Training

- Accelerated Payment of MGIB-AD

- Tuition Assistance Top-Up

- Tutorial Assistance Program

You can find out more about educational benefits and how to apply at **www.gibill.va.gov**. You can also call to ask about educational benefits at 800-827-1000.

Office of Special Education and Rehabilitative Services

At the Office of Special Education and Rehabilitative Services (OSERS), certain people with disabilities may apply for various programs that are designed to help them enter the workforce. According to the OSERS:

> The Office of Special Education and Rehabilitative Services (OSERS) understands the many challenges still facing individuals with disabilities and their families. Therefore, OSERS is committed to improving results and outcomes for people with disabilities of all ages. OSERS supports programs that serve millions of children, youth, and adults with disabilities.

The office is comprised of the Office of Special Education Programs (OSEP), the National Institute on Disability and Rehabilitation Research (NIDRR), and the Rehabilitation Services Administration (RSA).

According to the U.S. Department of Education, "Through the Office of the Assistant Secretary for Special Education and Rehabilitative Services, OSERS administers programs that support three institutions:

- The American Printing House for the Blind

- The National Technical Institute for the Deaf

- Gallaudet University

For more information, contact OSERS at 202-245-7486, or visit **www.ed.gov**.

The Office of Indian Education Programs

The Office of Indian Education Programs (OIEP) offers educational funds to eligible American Indian/Alaska Native students. According to the OIEP, they include:

- Higher ED Grants to assist those seeking a baccalaureate degree.

- Graduate Fellowship Grants: Designed to assist American Indian college graduates continuing their education at the master's, doctorate, and professional degree level.

- BIA Summer Law Program: American Indian students at the University of New Mexico have the opportunity to participate in a two-month program that prepares prospective lawyers for the rigors of law school.

For more information about these programs, and for eligibility requirements, visit **www.oiep.bia.edu**.

Wrapping It Up

Keep in mind that because these programs come from government, the rules can change. For example, in recent years rule changes have made it harder to become eligible for the Pell Grant. Yet, in 2006 more than 300,000 families became eligible for the new Academic Competitiveness Grants and the SMART grants, as these grants are new.

Grants are a great way to help pay for your college education, and you will not have to worry about paying it back. Your student loan payments will not be so hefty, and you will have fewer financial worries while in school as well.

Do not assume you are not qualified for a grant; always check with your school's financial aid office to see if you might be eligible. Generally, they will have much of the necessary paperwork to apply for government grants. For private grants, you might check out **www.fastweb.com**.

There are need-based and merit-based grants especially designed for women, minorities, military families, undergraduates, graduates, doctoral students, and more. Plus, there is money out there for veterans, and those with a disability. With a little research, you can no doubt find grants and other "free money" that you are eligible to receive.

Learn Now, Pay Later

$\mathcal{L}$et us face it, most college students end up taking out student loans, unless they are lucky enough to win the lottery, their parents are wealthy enough to cover the cost, or they receive grant money or a scholarship that covered the cost of tuition.

While student loans are a justifiable loan, meaning they make a lot of sense to take out since they are helping you attain a degree, they definitely have a few drawbacks. For one, with a student loan you can have hefty monthly payments and it could take years to pay it back. Writing out a check every month for $200, $250, $300, $400, or more can be a painful occurrence. You will have other financial obligations every month besides a student loan, such as a mortgage or rent payment, a car payment, utilities, gas, groceries, and so on, that can be difficult to pay on top of your student loan. Unless you are entering into a high-paying career (and very few careers pay well in the early years), you could be struggling, trying to make ends meet for years to come. What you do not want to do if you take out a student loan is take out more money that you really need to get through school. Sure, it may be nice to have the extra money at the time you are spending it, but loans are just that — they are loans. They are money you have to pay back, and there is no getting out of it. If you do not pay your student loans, you will ruin your credit, and you will become ineligible to borrow money for school ever again.

However, loans are a wonderful way to get through school. Many students could not consider going on to college if student loans were not available. Interest on student loans is about as low as it gets, so you cannot find a cheaper way to borrow money.

Interest rates are an important aspect of borrowing money, as is keeping the principal balance down to a minimum. That is, the money you borrowed in the first place.

To show how much interest rates affect payment and interest paid, consider a $20,000 loan that you will pay off in 5 years. At 18 percent interest, you will pay $500.36 per month with a grand total of $10,021.75 interest paid. That means an 18 percent interest rate will cost you an extra $10,021.75 over the life of the loan. Conversely, on that same $20,000 loan with an 8 percent interest rate, your payments will be $402.84, while the interest will cost you an extra $4,170.53. You will save about $6,000 in interest with a $20,000 loan if your interest rate is 8 percent instead of 18 percent. An 18 percent interest rate may seem high, but it is a going rate for many credit cards nowadays.

The rates on student loans, which we will learn more

about shortly, are generally in the 5 to 8 percent interest rate range. They are at a rate that you will not find easily anywhere else, so if you need to borrow money for college, take out a student loan. Just keep in mind the following:

- You should take only out what you truly need.

- You do not have to borrow the entire amount that is offered to you. You can lower the amount or decline the loan.

- You should figure out what your loan payments will be before you borrow.

- Make sure you estimate what your school costs will be so that you borrow the right amount.

- Read all the paperwork before you sign the loan.

- Compare interest rates on different loans.

- Find out if the loan you are taking out accrues interest while you are in school.

- See if there are any other ways to save. Some lenders cut the interest rate if you sign up for a monthly debit out of your checking or savings account to repay the loan.

To get started on your student loan, generally the first thing you will want to do is complete your FAFSA as described in Chapter 3. Now, let us explore student loans in more detail.

Federal Student Loan Programs

Two main federal programs are the largest source of college loans. One is the Federal Family Education Loan Program (FFELP) and the other one is the William D. Ford Federal Direct Loan Program (FDLP).

The programs offer subsidized loans and unsubsidized loans. Subsidized loans are based on financial need. The interest on subsidized loans will not accrue while you are in school at least half-time and during grace and authorized deferment periods. Unsubsidized loans are not need-based, and you are responsible for all of the interest that accrues on the loan, including while you are in school.

FFELP Loans

According to the U.S. Department of Education Web site, **www.ed.gov**, loan eligibility and loan type for a Federal Family Education Loan Program (FFELP) are as follows:

- **Stafford:** Individuals who are undergraduate, vocational, or graduate students accepted for enrollment at least half-time in participating schools.

- **Unsubsidized Stafford:** Individuals who are undergraduate, vocational, or graduate students accepted for enrollment at least half-time in participating schools.

- **PLUS:** Individuals who are parents of dependent undergraduate students accepted for enrollment at least half-time in participating schools. As of July 1, 2006, graduate students are also eligible.

- **Consolidation:** Individuals who have outstanding student loans and are in a grace period or repayment status, or those who have defaulted but have made satisfactory arrangements to repay their loan(s).

FFELP loans are available through many private banks, credit unions, and education finance companies, so you have a choice of lenders, but you might first ask your school's financial office first for their suggestions.

With the Federal Family Education Loan Program (FFELP), rates are very attractive in comparison to many loans. According to the U.S. Department of Education:

- With a Stafford loan, the government pays the interest when the student is in school and during periods of grace and deferment. The current interest rate as of July 1, 2006 was 6.8 percent.

- With an Unsubsidized Stafford loan, the interest is not paid by the government when the student is in school, nor during periods of grace and deferment. The current interest rate as of July 1, 2006 was 6.8 percent.

- With a PLUS loan, parents can borrow to pay the costs of higher education for their dependent undergraduates and graduate students to pay their costs. The current interest rate as of July 1, 2006 was 6.8 percent.

- With a Consolidation loan, more than one federal education loan is combined into a single loan. The current interest rate is figured by weighting the average of loans rounded upward to the nearest 1/8 percent. The interest rate was capped at 8.25 percent as of July 1, 2006.

When shopping around for a FFELP loan, you might want to consider what kind of customer service the lender offers. Also, do they have an online feature where you can access your loan and pay online? Will they pay any of the up-front fees for borrowers? Do they offer any discounts on the interest rates set by Congress?

FDLP Loans

According to the U.S. Department of Education, loan type and eligibility for the William D. Ford Federal Direct Loan Program (FDLP) is as follows:

- **Direct Stafford:** Individuals who are undergraduate, vocational, or graduate students accepted for enrollment at least half-time in participating schools.

- **Direct Unsubsidized Stafford**: Individuals who are undergraduate, vocational, or graduate students accepted for enrollment at least half-time in participating schools.

- **Direct PLUS:** Individuals who are parents of dependent undergraduate students accepted for enrollment at least half-time in participating schools. Beginning July 1, 2006, graduate students are also eligible.

- **Direct Consolidation:** Individuals who have outstanding student loans, or those who have defaulted but have made satisfactory arrangements to repay the loan(s) (or who agree to pay under the income contingent repayment plan).

With the William D. Ford Federal Direct Loan Program (FDLP), rates are very attractive in comparison to many loans. According to the U.S. Department of Education:

- With a Direct Stafford loan, the student is not liable for interest when in school and during periods of grace and deferment. The current interest rate as of July 1, 2006 was 6.8 percent.

- With a Direct Unsubsidized Stafford loan, the student is liable for interest while in school and during periods of grace and deferment. The current interest rate as of July 1, 2006 was 6.8 percent.

- With a Direct PLUS loan, parents can borrow to pay the costs of higher education for their dependent undergraduates and graduate students to pay their costs. The current interest rate as of July 1, 2006 was 7.9 percent.

- With a Direct Consolidation loan, more than one federal education loan is combined into a single loan. The current interest rate is figured by weighting the average of loans rounded upward to nearest 1/8 percent. The interest rate was capped at 8.25 percent as of July 1, 2006.

Before receiving your first Direct Loan, a Master Promissory

Note (MPN) must be signed. The MPN outlines the terms and conditions of your loan, and it is a legally binding agreement to repay your loan. Both the FAFSA and the MPN may be completed online.

To apply for a Direct Loan from the Department of Education, you must first complete your FAFSA as presented in Chapter 3. Your school's financial aid office may have the necessary paperwork, and you can complete the application online at **www.fafsa.ed.gov**.

Unlike other loans, borrowing is directly through the federal government, and loan payments are made to the Department of Education for the life of your loan. The loans are never sold. To save on interest, try to pay off your loans as quickly as possible.

Federal Perkins Loans

The Federal Perkins Loan Program is a loan program that provides low-interest (5 percent) loans to "exceptionally" needy students to help pay for the costs of postsecondary education. Nearly two thousand postsecondary (undergraduate, vocational, and graduate) institutions participate.

Your school determines which students have the greatest need, and then the school combines federal funds with some of the school's own funds for loans to qualifying students. Your school will either pay you directly (a minimum of two payments during the academic year), or apply your loan to your school charges. There are no fees with this loan. The average yearly award is $2,206, while the range is up to

$4,000 per year for undergraduates, and up to $6,000 per year for graduate students.

The requirements for a Federal Perkins loan are:

- You must be enrolled in an eligible school at least half-time in a degree program.

- You must have U.S. citizenship, permanent residency, or eligible noncitizen status.

- You must maintain satisfactory academic progress.

- You must not have any unresolved defaults or overpayments owed on Title IV education loans and grants.

- You must satisfy of all Selective Service requirements.

To apply for a Federal Perkins Loan, you must submit the Free Application for Federal Student Aid (FAFSA) at **www. fafsa.ed.gov**.

Federal Stafford Loans

You may have heard of "Stafford Loans" before, yet you may not know what kind of loan it is. In 1988, Congress renamed the Federal Guaranteed Student Loan program the Robert T. Stafford Student Loan program, in honor of Senator Robert Stafford of Vermont for his work in higher education.

Stafford loans refer to the Federal Direct Student Loan

Program (FDSLP, also known as Direct Loans), granted directly from the United States Department of Education and the Federal Family Education Loan Program (FFELP), available from a private lender.

Stafford loans are guaranteed by the full faith of the U.S. Government, and they are offered at a lower interest rate than the borrower would otherwise be able to get for a private loan. This means if the student defaults the lender is paid by the government. There are strict eligibility requirements and borrowing limits on Stafford loans.

With a Stafford loan, you are receiving either a subsidized (the government pays the interest while you are in school) or unsubsidized (you pay all the interest, but the payments may be deferred until after graduation) loan.

To receive a subsidized Stafford loan, financial need must be demonstrated on your FAFSA. Most subsidized Stafford loans are awarded to students with a family AGI of under $50,000. All students are generally eligible for the unsubsidized Stafford loan. You can apply for and receive both kinds of loans. Currently the interest rate is 6.8 percent. It is the rate you should receive from whatever source your get the loan. Check to see if discounts for electronic loan payments, or other discounts, are available. The loan fee is 4 percent, which is deducted from your disbursement check, and generally the repayment terms are ten years, but other terms, such as extended payment terms, are available.

So How Much Can You Borrow?

According to **www.findaid.com**,

> As of July 1, 2007, Stafford Loans allow dependent undergraduates to borrow up to $3,500 their freshman year (up from $2,625), $4,500 their sophomore year (up from $3,500) and $5,500 for each remaining year (independent students and students whose parents have been turned down for a PLUS loan can borrow an additional unsubsidized $4,000 the first two years and $5,000 the remaining years). Graduate students can borrow $20,500 per year (up from $18,500), although only $8,500 of that is subsidized. There are also cumulative limits of $23,000 for an undergraduate education and a $65,500 combined limit for undergraduate and graduate. (For independent students and for students whose parents were denied a PLUS loan the cumulative limits are $46,000 and $138,500, respectively. Some medical school students may be able to borrow up to $40,500 a year (up from $38,500) and $189,125 total.)

When applying for a Stafford loan, you must first complete a Free Application for Federal Student Aid (FAFSA) at **www.fafsa.ed.gov**.

Federal PLUS Loans

The Federal PLUS loan is a parent loan program for parents of undergraduate students that offers an affordable, low-interest solution for parents to help out their dependent children. Independent students are not eligible. Banks and other lending institutions offer these loans.

The loan is not based on household income, assets, or financial need, so most parents are eligible to receive the loan. The loan can be used to cover 100 percent of the cost of education, minus any financial awards already awarded to the student. For instance, if a student received a scholarship for $2,500, that may be deducted from the loan amount that parents can receive. The total amount can, however, include tuition as well as books, food, housing, supplies, and other expenses that are intrinsic to attending school.

A few facts about a Federal PLUS loan:

- You must be a U.S. citizen or national, a U.S. permanent resident, or eligible noncitizen.

- A credit check is required.

- Collateral is not required.

- The federal government does not require that you file the Free Application for Federal Student Aid (FAFSA) to qualify for a Parent PLUS loan, but schools do require the FAFSA for Parent PLUS borrowers. Check with your school's financial aid office.

- For loans first disbursed on or after July 1, 2006, the interest is fixed at 8.5 percent.

- The federal government charges a 3 percent origination fee.

- Payments may be postponed while you child is attending school.

- Interest may be tax deductible. Check with your tax advisor.

Check with your lender about specific details, and about applying for the loan.

Parents of graduate students can apply for the Graduate PLUS loan, another low-interest, federally backed student loan guaranteed by the U.S. government. Just like with the Parent PLUS Loan, the loan can be used to pay for the total cost of education, including supplies, books, and even food, minus any financial awards already awarded to the student. Students can postpone repayment of their federal student loans while enrolled at least half-time in a degree or certificate program. Banks and other lending institutions offer these loans.

Repayment terms of PLUS loans are the same as what is outlined in this chapter under Repayment. Options include: Standard repayment, graduated repayment, income-sensitive repayment, and extended repayment.

Service-Cancelable Loans

A service-cancelable loan is just that. You provide a service upon completing school, and your school loan may be cancelled. You must generally work in a "critical need" field for a set number of years. The loans are funded through the government. "Mapping Your Future" has list of opportunities to get your loan cancelled by providing service. The opportunities for these loans range from having 70 percent of your loan cancelled by volunteering in Vista or the Peace Corps, to teaching in elementary or secondary schools in a low-income school district and having $5,000 to $17,500 cancelled from your student loan debt. The site below links to an Annual Directory of Designated Low-Income Schools for Teacher Cancellation Benefits. You might also check with your school's financial aid office to see if they have any service-cancelable loan possibilities.

Let us look at a few of the Service-cancelable loan possibilities that are listed **www.mapping-your-future.org**.

Child Care Providers

Certain child care providers who have outstanding federal student loans may be eligible to have their loans forgiven — in other words, you will not have to repay the amount. To be eligible for loan forgiveness, all of the following criteria must be met:

- You must be a new borrower as of Oct. 1, 1998, (i.e., have no outstanding balance on a Federal Family Education Loan [FFEL] Program or Federal Direct Program loan as of that date).

- You must have obtained an associate's or bachelor's degree in early childhood education from an institution of higher education. If you originally received a degree in another area of study, but later obtained a degree in early childhood education, forgiveness will be limited to eligible loans you obtained for a maximum of two of the academic years required to obtain the early childhood education degree.

- You must have worked full-time as a child care provider in a facility that serves a low-income community for the two consecutive years preceding the year during which you requested loan forgiveness. At least 70 percent of the individuals that facility serves must be from families that earn less than 85 percent of the state median household income.

- You must not have received benefits for the same child care service under the National and Community Service Act of 1990 (AmeriCorps).

The program is offered on a first-come, first-serve basis, subject to the availability of funds.

Forgiveness Amounts

To be eligible for forgiveness, you must maintain full-time employment for successive, uninterrupted 12-month periods. A proportion of the balance of your FFEL Program or Federal Direct Loans (including interest that accrues) may be forgiven in the following increments:

- 20 percent after completing two consecutive years of qualifying employment

- 20 percent after completing the third consecutive year of qualifying employment

- 30 percent after completing the fourth consecutive year of qualifying employment

- 30 percent after completing the fifth consecutive year of qualifying employment

Law Enforcement or Corrections Officer

Your loan will be cancelled if you serve full-time as a qualifying law enforcement or corrections officer. To establish eligibility, the school must determine that your:

- Employing agency is eligible; i.e., a local, state, or federal agency that is publicly funded and its activities pertain to crime prevention, control, or reduction or to the enforcement of the criminal law, and

- Position is essential to the agency's primary mission; i.e., you are a sworn officer or person whose principal responsibilities are unique to the criminal justice system.

Repayment

With many types of loans, you have several repayment options to choose from: standard, extended, graduated, and income contingent. The options can sometimes be changed any time during the life of the loan, so if you start with a standard repayment plan, and run into financial hardships along the way, you can find out about an income-contingent repayment plan. You should always find out about payment plans before you agree to any loan. Always find out what the plan options are, and whether they can be changed. Check with your lender for specific details before agreeing to accept a loan.

Here is an overview of what the repayment plans typically are:

- **Standard Plan:** A fixed payment every month (generally at least $50) and you have (typically) ten years to repay your loan.

- **Extended Plan:** A fixed payment every month (generally at least $50), but you have (typically) 12 to 30 years to repay your loan.

- **Graduated Plan:** Payments start out low then increase (generally every two years). You have (typically) up to 30 years to repay the loan.

- **Income-Contingent Repayment Plan:** Each year, your monthly payments will be based of your adjusted gross income (AGI, plus your spouse's income if you are married), family size, and the total amount of your loan.

You can also inquire from your lender about a Student Loan Consolidation.

With loan consolidation, your eligible student loans will be consolidated into a new loan with a single monthly payment and a fixed interest rate. Your monthly payments may lower, but sometimes with a higher total loan cost with consideration of extra fees.

If you run into financial hardship, return to school at least part-time, are on active duty during war, national emergency, or military operation, or encounter other serious hardships, you may request a period of deferment, so you can temporarily postpone payment of your loan. Keep in mind that you must apply and be approved for a deferment. Different loans have different deferment requirements; always contact your lender directly about a deferment.

You can also request what is called "forbearance." You can reduce your monthly loan payment should you be approved for one. The length of the loan is extended for forbearances. Often the amount of time it takes to repay your loan is extended.

If you run into any trouble making payments on your loan, try to work something out with the lender. Generally, you can reach a doable agreement so that your loan does not default and you do not ruin your credit. Work something out with the lender as soon as you can. It is better not to wait until you miss a payment to make the call. Lenders are more apt to work with you if you call early and do not have a habit of being late with your payments.

There are certain circumstances allowing your student loan to be discharged, including the event of your death, if you become totally and permanently disabled after the loan is disbursed, if the school you were attending closed, in certain bankruptcy cases, or if your loan was falsely certified by an eligible school, such as signing your name without permission. You can find out more about loan discharges at the U.S. Department of Education Web site, **www.ed.gov**.

Private Loans

After you have exhausted all of your federal borrowing

option first, you may find you still need more funds. That is why some are turning to private loans in order to fill the gaps. Private loans are loans that are procured from a bank, a lending institution, or even a credit card. Interest rates on private school loans are often credit based, meaning the better the credit, the lower the interest. Before you (or your parents) consider taking out a private loan, plenty of research needs to be done. Here are some of the questions you should find out the answer to before you agree to the loan:

- What is the interest rate?

- Is the interest rate fixed or variable?

- What are the fees?

- What are the repayment options?

- What are the borrower benefits, such as discounts, customer service, and online servicing?

- Is there a prepayment penalty?

It is a good idea to read all of the loan documents you are agreeing to. Do not sign anything unless you fully understand what you are signing. There may be hidden fees and clauses that you may not notice at first. All lenders have different requirements.

You might first ask your school's financial aid department if they have a list of private loan lenders, or ask at your bank or your parents' bank if they have private school loans available.

One more source to try for a private loan is through your family. If you can, you might ask a relative or your parents if you can "borrow" money from them. You could work out a loan agreement that is similar to what you may have gotten from a government loans, with low interest and payments over an extended time. Or you could offer to make them a deal they cannot turn down, such as an offer to pay them higher rates than they may have gotten elsewhere. Otherwise, you could ask your relatives, or parents, if they could consider it as an advanced inheritance. You could work out an arrangement that they pay the school directly, and even fill out a loan agreement with the terms spelled out.

If it is a gift, there is good news. A tax-free gift of up to $10,000 per year may given, as it is called an "annual exclusion." Always check with your financial advisor before making assumptions about gifting and tax savings.

Bank Loans

You have several options when getting a private loan for undergraduate, graduate, law, dental, or medical school studies. Some of the loans can be for as little as $1,000, while others can go up to over $200,000. Many private bank loans offer repayment options. As with other loans, you should shop around and find one that best suits your needs.

One of the loans that is available through banks and some private lenders is a TERI loan. TERI, The Education Resources Institute, Inc., describes itself as "the most experienced and largest nonprofit sponsor of private loans for education. TERI is also a leader in providing college access programs that help people identify and achieve their postsecondary goals."

With a TERI loan you can borrow, on an annual basis, up to the cost of your schooling, minus any other aid you are receiving, such as grants, loans, and scholarships. The loans are designed for undergraduate, graduate, continuing education, health profession, medical residency, and more. They offer competitive rates. Often the minimum loan amount is $1,000, and it can rise as high as a several hundred thousand dollars when seeking funding for medial school.

You generally must have a satisfactory credit history, while your employment history and current income must meet established criteria as set forth by the lender. Depending on the level of schooling you are seeking, the annual amount and income and employment requirements vary. Repayment options vary according to the lender.

Some of the other requirements may or may not include:

- You must be attending a TERI-approved school.

- You must be enrolled at least half-time.

- You might need a qualified U.S. cosigner.

You can apply for a TERI loan at **www.teri.org**, or you can apply at your bank.

Many banks offer TERI loans in addition to other types of school loans. Here are a few:

Bank of America offers an Education Maximizer® loan

designed to help students cover unexpected college cost. They also offer a CampusEdge® student loan that is designed for undergraduate students who are looking to supplement federal loans and other financial aid. You can find out more at **www.bankofamerica.com**.

Wachovia Bank offers a Wachovia Individual Education Loan that is designed for qualified undergraduates and graduate students to cover 100 percent of their total cost of attendance, less other aid received. You can find out more at **www.wachovia.com**.

SunTrust Bank offers an Academic Answer® loan for undergraduate and graduate studies. You can borrow up to $75,000 for undergraduate study, and $150,000 for graduate study. The annual maximum is $45,000, or your school's cost of attendance, whichever is less. You can find out more at **http://moneyforcollege.suntrust.com**.

Many banks offer their own student loan programs. It is best to start with your own bank to see what they might offer for student loans. Loan types and terms vary. Make sure you read and understand all of your loan documents before agreeing to a loan. Always inquire about the following:

- Find out what the fees are.

- Understand what the repayment terms are.

- Know what the interest rate is.

- Find out when your payments begin.

- Know what your payments will be.

- Learn where the loan funds go — directly to you? Or the school?

Home Equity Alternatives

If you have home equity, or your parents do, you can consider home equity as a source for funding college.

So what is home equity? Home equity is the portion of your home's value that you own, versus what the lender owns. For instance, if you home's fair market value is $200,000 and your outstanding loan on your home totals $130,000, that would mean you have $70,000 in home equity.

Home equity is a valuable asset that you can tap into for funds, and you do not have to sell you home in order to get the money. Your home is your collateral for the loan. However, if you default on a home equity loan, your lender could foreclose on your home. Yes, you could lose the home if you do not make your loan payments.

Home equity loans generally have some fees. There are fees for closing costs, for setting up the loan, applying for the loan, recording the loan, and performing a property survey and title search, as well as other fees. Often the repayment terms are anywhere from five to 20 years, depending on the amount you borrowed. If you sell you home, the loan must be paid back in full.

There are two basic types of home equity loans:

- **Term Equity Loan:** A lump sum, fixed-interest-rate loan with the same payments every month.

- **Home Equity Line of Credit:** You borrow what you need, and generally pay a variable interest rate.

When your payment time expires, you must pay off the balance, or apply to extend or renew the loan or line of credit. Fees vary depending on the lender.

You can receive a home equity loan or line of credit from a variety of lenders and banks. They do not have to be the originator of any of your previous loans. For instance, you can have a first home loan with ABC Lender and get a home equity loan from XYZ Bank.

While your parents can borrow money against their home, they may want to consider downsizing their home instead. If the market is right, and they are looking for a smaller residence anyway, maybe now is the time to sell and use some of the funds to help pay for your college education. Besides freeing up some cash, there are capital gains to consider. Capital gains on personal real estate are tax free up to $500,000 for couples and $250,000 for singles, with certain restrictions, such as living in the property for a certain amount of years. Ask your tax advisor for details. That means you can make that much on a real estate sale, without paying hefty capital gains taxes. Not only that, moving to a smaller residence can help save on your overall expenses, such as maintenance, insurance, utilities, and taxes.

Retirement Fund Borrowing

One of the last places you or your parents should look for college funding is in your retirement plan. Before tapping into a retirement fund, it is a good idea to have exhausted all of your other resources. You should have applied for every grant and scholarship that you can, taken advantage of student loans and private loans, and checked into home equity before dipping into a 401(k).

If you must borrow from your or your parents' 401(k) plan, keep in mind that certain tax rules limit the amount you can use as a loan. Tax advantages are not available such as with certain other loans, like a home equity loan where you can deduct the interest. With retirement fund borrowing, you can typically borrow up to 50 percent of your vested account balance or $50,000 — whichever is less. Although you do not have to qualify for the loan, as it is money you are borrowing from yourself, remember when the money is taken out it is no longer earning money for your or your parents' retirement. It is that much less money that is in an income-earning account.

Before you take any money out of a 401(k) plan, you should always:

- Check the interest rate on the loan against your 401(k).

- Find out about an early withdrawal penalty if you do not pay the loan back. It may be as large as 10 percent.

- Do not assume your 401(k) plan allows for loans, though most do.

- Find out what the repayment terms are.

It is best to speak with a tax advisor first. Taking money out of your retirement account can end up costing you more than you anticipated if you do not know the guidelines for how much money you can borrow against your 401(k) for your particular situation.

Keep in mind that you should never borrow any money that is going to put your own retirement, or your parents' retirement, in jeopardy. While they may want to pitch in to help their child, or you may feel that your parents "owe" you, the later years of life need to be planned as well. Heading into retirement years with nothing in the bank is a bad financial move. While your parents may be able to help you out with college, you need to keep their own financial situation in mind. You should try to exhaust other resources first.

Wrapping It Up

Your best bet for finding a good rate on a student loan is through one of the several government student loan programs. Certain careers and schools offer opportunities for service-cancelable loans. That means that under certain circumstances, like teaching in a low-income area for a specified amount of years, you will not have to pay the loan back, or at least part of the loan. Home equity loans are a possible loan source if you or your parents have equity in a home. Retirement borrowing against your 401(k) can be possible, but check with your tax advisor before you consider taking out any money from your retirement savings. Borrowing from your nest egg is usually something to consider last. To make extra income you can work either during the school year or during the summer months while you may not be in school. Remember, the less money that you have to borrow, the better.

Work It Out!

Even with grants, scholarships, and loans, sometimes it is a good idea to supplement your college years with extra work. Working off some of your college costs can reduce your need for more loans. Remember, loans are money that you have to start paying back generally six months after graduation. Besides lowering your loan money, work opportunities give you helpful training so that when you graduate you will have some experience in your field. Once you are done with school and looking for a job, having that extra edge of experience is helpful in landing a better job sooner. In addition, working while in school can provide you with a contact base that will be helpful for you to tap into when you are looking for a career. For instance, you may have a summer job and your manager suddenly receives a higher position at a better company — a company that you always wanted to work for. Well, now you personally know someone who works there, and they might be able to help you get in the door. Let us look at some of the opportunities you can exploit to work your way through college.

CASE STUDY: SHAUN FAWCETT

Shaun Fawcett, M.B.A.

Final Draft Publications

5-1501 Notre-Dame W.

Montreal, QC, H3C 1L2, Canada

Phone: (514) 989-1698

e-mail: findraft@sympatico.ca

http://www.writinghelp-central.com

http://www.writinghelptools.com

Ten Tips for Writing a Winning Resume

1. Keep It Focused and Businesslike

A resume should be specific and all business. Remember, you are asking an employer to invest significant time and money by choosing you over other similarly qualified people.

2. More Than Two Pages Is Too Much

For students, recent graduates, or people with just a few years of experience, try to keep your resume to one page, two as an absolute maximum.

3. Get the Words and Punctuation Right

Make sure the grammar, spelling, and punctuation in your resume are perfect. Keep the language clear and simple. If you draft it yourself, have someone with excellent writing skills do an editorial review and a careful proofread. Refer to an English language "style guide" to double-check.

4. Read Between the Lines

Customize the resume to match the stated requirements of the job that you are applying for, without being misleading. Review and analyze the job ad carefully. Itemize the key

CASE STUDY: SHAUN FAWCETT

qualifications, skills, and abilities the employer is seeking. When possible, study the company's annual report and Web site, and weave the themes and terms found there into your resume and cover letter.

5. Make Sure It Looks Good

Use a crisp, clean, simple presentation format for a professional-looking resume. Just a bit of simple line work and/or shading will do the trick. If you need help, ask your friends, or you may wish to seek professional advice.

6. Show What You Can Do Today

Focus first on your recent experience that is most relevant to the position at hand. Less relevant and/or dated experience should be either eliminated or summarized in brief point form near the end of your resume.

7. Be a Straight Shooter

Be completely honest. When people lie or "creatively exaggerate" on their resume, they are almost invariably exposed, sooner or later. Think about it — who really wants to get a job based on a lie(s) and then have to live in fear of eventually being found out?

8. Follow the Instructions

Submit your resume in exactly the form that the prospective employer requests. If they say e-mail, fax, or snail mail, send it that way. If using snail mail, use the complete address that they specify, so it arrives in the right location.

9. Do Not Get Lost in the Mail

Be careful to respect certain conventions that the prospective employer may require in your resume. For example, make sure that the cover letter mentions the exact name of the specific position you are applying for, and the competition number, if applicable.

10. Do Not Repeat Yourself

In the cover letter, do not repeat what is already detailed in the body of the resume. Introduce yourself first, then briefly summarize why you believe that you have the qualifications and experience to fulfill the duties of the position. Express enthusiasm. Close by stating how you are looking forward to hearing more from them soon, and that you will follow up if necessary.

Work and Service Opportunities

If you are looking to land work during college, you might want to check the college bulletin to see if any opportunities are posted. Another good source is to check in the local papers under the want ads. Temporary work and even long-term opportunities can be found through temporary agencies such as Kelly Services (**www.kellyservices.us)** and Manpower, Inc., (**www.us.manpower.com)**. Although temp agencies may specialize in temporary work, certainly they offer permanent jobs as well. Some of the temp agencies allow you to apply for work online— although an initial interview may be required. Many businesses advertise for help with "Help Wanted" signs in their windows, while other, larger companies have ongoing needs for new employees year-round. Some of the jobs are better preparations for after graduation, so you might want to consider trying to find any work you can in your field. For instance, accounting students may look for seasonal tax work at H&R Block, while law students may want to seek work in a law library.

The federal government also offers a Federal Work-Study (FWS) program; a need-based employment program for full-time undergraduate, graduate, and professional students. According to the U.S. Department of Education, "The FWS Program provides funds that are earned through part-time employment to assist students in financing the costs of post-secondary education." This federally funded program is offered at approximately 3,400 participating post-secondary institutions. Hourly wages must not be less than the federal minimum wage. Jobs are often posted at the school's campus or on the school's Web site. You can find out more about the Federal Work-Study program at **www.ed.gov**; ask your financial aid office for more details and Federal Work-Study possibilities at your school.

Service opportunities are also something to consider. Service opportunities play a role in providing service to the community, with work opportunities through agencies such as the United Way, the American Red Cross, and Habitat for Humanity. Other service opportunities can be found in local theaters, groups, or even churches. Service opportunities can be geared toward your major. For instance, a theater major may find that working for a local theater makes sense, while nursing students may benefit from working with the Red Cross. Some of the service opportunities are unpaid positions, while others give small stipends. You might ask your college if academic credit can be earned with a service opportunity. Either way, service opportunities provide great benefits to the community.

Something to consider before figuring out what job suits you during college is to conduct an information interview. That is where you meet with people who are already working in your chosen career and ask questions about particular occupations or companies. This gives you a personal perspective on what the job would entail, plus it does not hurt to make a career contact.

You might want to try job shadowing. Job shadowing is where you visit a business and observe one or more positions at work, whether for an hour or a day. This again gives you the benefit of understanding a position more, while offering you an opportunity to make another contact.

Getting early experience in your career helps you out in many ways, such as:

- **Earning money:** You are earning some money even with part-time jobs.

- **Resume building:** You are gaining some work experience, which is good for your resume.

- **Getting your feet wet:** You may be learning about your field before you finish school.

- **Networking:** You may be making contacts that will help later on with your job search.

- **Learning skills:** You are learning new skills from knowing how to work as a team to learning how to do something.

When looking for a job, and even after you have found one, remember to:

- Keep your resume up-to-date.

- Start to build a network. Get names and numbers of those whom you might contact later.

- Get your letters of recommendation. It is easier to get them now, rather than backtrack.

- If applicable, start to build your portfolio. Make sure you get copies of what you have worked on.

To find a job, try the following:

- Check the want ads.

- Ask at your school's career center.

- Look at bulletin boards.

- Go to job fairs.

- Ask friends, family, and fellow students if they have heard of anything available.

- Make cold calls. Either call businesses or stop in and fill out an application.

- Sign up at temp agencies. Sometimes temp jobs turn into longer jobs.

- Register with an agency in person and/or online.

Cooperative Education

Cooperative education combines secondary education with work experience that is practical for the focus of your studies. You receive academic credit and pay that varies according to your major, the employer, the job's location, the position, and your qualifications for the job. Often the programs are designed to have you alternate semesters of academic study with semesters of full-time employment in positions related to your academic or career interests, although there are other situations. Some colleges offer programs with cooperative education, other do not, while others focus entirely on cooperative education. For instance, NC State University, the largest university in North Carolina, has 12 colleges with most major academic disciplines.

According to NC State University, "We integrate the opportunities our world-class research programs offer students into our degree tracks and emphasize innovation and on-the-job experience. Instruction at NC State begins in the classroom, but it almost always leads into laboratories — where students work side-by-side with leading researchers in their fields — or to stages, galleries, and off-campus job internships and co-ops that expose students to real-world challenges and experiences. By the time most NC State students graduate, they have not only mastered their area of expertise, they have gained valuable job experience (and often job offers) and discovered the potential for inquiry and creativity within themselves." For more information, contact **www.ncsu.edu**.

NC State's program is a great way to get started in your career while gaining school credit along the way.

Another school whose focus is cooperative education is the University of North Texas, which offers undergraduate and graduate degrees in everything from aerospace studies to business and political science.

According to the university, "Most programs offer hands-on experience in your field before graduation. Internships provide invaluable training and a head start on your career. UNT's nationally accredited Cooperative Education program provides students with paid, supervised positions related to their field of study, often for several semesters. Some students even receive academic credit for their work and/or permanent job offers after graduation." For more information, visit **www.unt.edu**.

Some of the benefits with receiving a cooperative education are:

- Practical experience in your field of study.

- Your education is applied to real-life work situations.

- You make useful contacts.

- You learn real-life working skills.

- You earn money.

A great source of information about cooperative education is with the National Commission for Cooperative Education. According to the Commission, "The National Commission for Cooperative Education (NCCE) is dedicated to advancing cooperative education throughout the United States. Since 1962, the Commission and its college and business partners have supported the development of quality work-integrated learning programs through: National Advocacy, Executive Outreach, Public Awareness, Students & Parent Response Center, and Research & Education."

The Commission developed a co-op model to define what cooperative education should consist of. The characteristics for this model, as detailed on their Web site, are:

- Formal recognition by the school as an educational strategy integrating classroom learning and progressive work experiences, with a constructive academic relationship between teaching faculty and co-op faculty or administrators.

- Structure for multiple work experiences in formalized sequence with study leading to degree completion of an academic program.

- Work experiences, which include both an appropriate learning environment and productive work. Work experiences related to career or academic goals. Formal recognition of the co-op experience on student records (e.g. grade, credit hours, part of degree requirement, notation on transcript, etc.). Pre-employment preparation for students, as well as ongoing advising.

- Agreement among the school, employer, and the student on:

  - Job description and new learning opportunities.

  - Specified minimum work periods (equivalent in length to an academic term (quarter, semester, or trimester). In alternating programs, students work approximately 40 hours per week, full-time during the term. In parallel programs, students work approximately 20 hours per week, part-time during the term.

  - Work monitored by the school and supervised by employers.

  - Official school enrollment during employment.

  - Recognition as a co-op employee by the employer.

  - Evaluations by the student, the school, and the employer, with guided reflection by the student.

- Remuneration for the work performed.

- Provision for employer and school evaluation of quality and relevance of the work experience and curriculum designed to maximize outcomes for students, employers, and the school.

You can find out more about the Commission at **www.co-op.edu**.

Internships

One way to gain work experience in your field of study, as well as perhaps receiving academic credit for the hours spent working, is with internships. Internships are approved and monitored work experience that is related to your field of study and that meets learning goals. With some internships you can receive academic credit, while with others you will not. To receive credit for your internship, you generally have to get the internship approved beforehand by your school. Some schools have an office that is in charge of helping to find internships for students. However, even if you school does not offer academic credit for internships, or if they do not assist you with finding an internship, they may be worth pursuing on your own. Some of the benefits of internships include:

- You will gain a deeper understanding about a career.

- You will have work experience in your field once you graduate.

- You will be able to find out if you are pursuing the right career.

- You will learn valuable skills.

- You will make connections and start to network.

- If you are planning to go to graduate school, you have an extra edge on your application.

Before you figure out how to get an internship, you might first try to figure out what kind of internship interests you and what you hope to gain from your internship. Also figure out what kind of company you would like to work for. Is it a large company or a small one? Ask yourself if you will only take a paid internship, or if you are willing to work in an unpaid position. Also ask yourself how long of an internship you are interested in.

Once you have pondered what you want from an internship, then you have to find one. You might first ask your school counselor if they know where to look. There may be plenty of resources at your school to help you find an internship, from a bulletin board with a listing, to their Web site, to an internship advisor on staff. You could always try to tap your family and friends for internship possibilities. Perhaps your uncle works for a company you are interested in interning at; why not give him a call? There are also Web sites such as Monster Trak (**www.monstertrak.monster. com**) or VAULT, (**www.vault.com**) with internship listings. You can always research the company you are interested in and see if they have something posted on their Web site about internships and who to contact. You might also try local career fairs, as some companies have information about internships available at fairs and other recruitment events.

Always make sure to find out if you can get college credit for your internship. Your school counselor/advisor should know if that is possible.

College Work Programs

If you are interested in working while in school, you can apply for a variety of programs at your school that are designed to enhance your education.

The Federal Work-Study Program (FWS) was formerly known as the College Work-Study Program. According to the U.S. Department of Education:

> The FWS Program provides funds that are earned through part-time employment to assist students in financing the costs of postsecondary education. Students can receive FWS funds at approximately 3,400 participating postsecondary institutions. Institutional financial aid administrators at participating institutions have substantial flexibility in determining the amount of FWS awards to provide to students who are enrolled or accepted for enrollment. Hourly wages must not be less than the federal minimum wage.

The Federal Work-Study Program (FWS) helps you contribute to your education by enhancing already-acquired skills and learning new skills while employed either on-campus or in a community service role.

Generally the process to apply for a work-study program is to complete the FAFSA, as described in Chapter 3, and then complete an application at your school, should they offer this program. You must maintain academic success, as defined by your school, in order to participate in this program while you attend school.

In addition to the Federal Work-Study Program (FWS), certain schools offer their own program designed for those that are not eligible for the FWS. Depending on the school, opportunities may be posted for students to apply for, or students propose their own jobs at the school and see if they can receive approval for a position. Some schools have work-study coordinators in charge of work-study programs, while others may have less structure to how work-study programs are procured. Some require that you maintain a certain GPA. Below are a few work-study scenarios.

At Sterling College in Vermont, **http://www.sterlingcollege. edu**, the College Work Program requires that you work on-campus while attending school:

> In addition to fulfilling academic responsibilities, students function as integral members of the work force of the college. They are employed an average of six hours a week in one of 50 different jobs in the Work College Program. In exchange for work, students are eligible to earn a minimum $1,450 in tuition and book credit. Many students earn more than that amount by doing additional work. For example, students may be awarded an additional $500 tuition credit matched by income earned on their off-campus internships.

Sterling College
P.O. Box 72
Craftsbury Common, VT 05827
General Information 800-648-3591

Loyola University New Orleans offers a College Work Study (CWS) that "is a federal financial aid work program funded by Loyola University and the United States Department of Education." You can find paid work-study opportunities at **www.loyno.edu/human.resources/work.study**. The jobs each pay $7 per hour, and most jobs average about ten hours per week. Students must first complete their FAFSA, while a College Work Study Coordinator assists with helping you participate in the program.

Loyola University New Orleans
6363 St. Charles Avenue
New Orleans, Louisiana 70118
Office of Admissions 504-865-3240
or 800-4-LOYOLA

Alderson-Broaddus College offers the Job Book, located online, that has a listing of all possible job openings, as well as an explanation of how to apply for them. You may earn up to $1,400 a year ($700 per semester) for the federal/college work program. You must complete your FAFSA first, and you are then awarded a work program by the financial aid office. You can find out more at **www.ab.edu**.

Alderson-Broaddus College
101 College Hill Drive

Philippi, WV 26416
Office of Admissions 800-263-1549

At Mount Carmel College of Nursing, you can participate in their College Work Program and earn $6.70 per hour for up to ten hours per week. You must apply for the program with the financial aid office. For more information, visit **www.mccn.edu**.

Mount Carmel College of Nursing
127 S. Davis Avenue
Columbus, OH 43222
General Information (614) 234-5800
or 800-556-6942

At Columbia College in Chicago, Illinois, you can take advantage of the federal work-study program. According to the college,

The Student Financial Services (SFS) Office awards FWS to eligible students each year who demonstrate financial need on the Free Application for Federal Student Aid (FAFSA).

FWS will appear on the Financial Aid Award Letter from SFS. Students may not earn more than the FWS award amount that appears on the award letter. The funds are not applied to the student's account. The majority of work-study jobs are on-campus. Some students may work for non-profit organizations in the FWS Community Service Program.

FWS is not a grant. Students must get a job to earn the award. The Student Employment Office will assist students in finding a work-study job. All students must have the proper identification documents to complete a job application in the Student Employment Office.

Columbia College
600 S. Michigan Avenue
Chicago, IL 60605
312-344-7260
www.colum.edu

Ask your academic advisor if there are work-study opportunities at your school, as it is great way to earn money while you learn and many positions are right on campus.

Americorps/National Service

Take advantage of an opportunity to work for AmeriCorps and you could earn a Segal AmeriCorps Education Award of $4,725 to pay for college, graduate school, or even to pay back qualified student loans. While you work for AmeriCorps you are helping those across the country in community service positions. According to AmeriCorps, the positions range from the chance to:

- Tutor and mentor disadvantaged youth

- Fight illiteracy

- Improve health services

- Build affordable housing

- Teach computer skills

- Clean parks and streams

- Manage or operate after-school programs

- Help communities respond to disasters

- Build organizational capacity

You are paid a "modest living allowance during service, and once you complete your service you can apply for the Segal AmeriCorps Education Award."

There are several programs that you can apply for, including the AmeriCorps State and National that offers national projects in every state, U.S. territory, and on tribal reservations. There is also AmeriCorps VISTA, a national service program designed specifically to fight poverty. The AmeriCorps NCCC (National Civilian Community Corps), a residential program for men and women age 18 to 24. According the AmeriCorps: "In partnership with nonprofit organizations, state and local agencies, and faith-based and other community organizations, members complete service projects throughout the region they are assigned."

You can apply for AmeriCorps and find out more about the Segal AmeriCorps Education Award at **www.americorps.gov**.

In addition to helping communities, you are adding great experience for your resume, plus getting a chance to receive a scholarship for your education.

Reserves/National Guard

If you have thought about joining the National Guard, or the Reserves, you may be pleased to hear about their program College First, which is designed to allow you to attend undergrad or graduate school full-time, all while earning over $2,000 per month, with a guarantee of no deployment during your first two years of Guard service. According to the National Guard, "The program also includes many financial benefits that could potentially pay for your entire education."

The National Guard states that you are eligible if:

- You have no experience in the military.

- You are a high school graduate or graduating senior.

- You score 50 or higher on the Armed Services Vocational Aptitude Battery (ASVAB).

- You agree to complete Advanced Individual Training (AIT) immediately following Basic Training.

- You are accepted by a U.S. Department of Education-accredited college or university within 90 days of completing AIT.

- You remain a student in good standing for the duration of your nondeployment period.

- You meet all other National Guard enlistment Standards.

What Do You Get?

- Up to two years of nondeployment following completion of Initial Active Duty Training (IADT).

- An enlistment bonus of up to $20,000.

- The Montgomery G.I. Bill — Selected Reserve (MGIB-SR), basic educational assistance of $309 per month.

- The MGIB-SR Kicker — additional educational assistance of $350 per month (available to those enlisting in a critical MOS and assigned to a qualified unit).

- 100% tuition assistance, up to $4,500 per year.

- Up to 100% state tuition assistance; amount varies by state.

* *Recruiting Assistant Pay (Voluntary): This is a 100% optional, performance-based program, open to Guard members to assist in helping recruit for your unit. Recruiting Assistants (RAs) can earn additional income assisting Guard recruiting efforts, by identifying well-qualified men and women for service in the ARNG. RAs earn $2,000 for each new recruit who enlists and reports to Basic Training, or for each prior service member who affiliates with a unit for four months. Monthly dollar amount is based on one referral enlisting each quarter.*

The Army National Guard funds up to 100 percent of tuition

costs and fees, not to exceed $250 per semester hour and will be limited to $4500 per person per fiscal year.

Contact your local recruiter for details about College First in your state. Or visit **www.1800goguard.com** to find out more about the Reserves or the National Guard and what college benefits are available to you.

Wrapping It Up

A great way to lower your college costs is by working off some of the costs. There are plenty of ways you can do so, from work-study opportunities, to internships, to cooperative education. If you are inclined to join the National Guard, or Reserves, you might find that they offer several ways to help you pay for college. Paying for college along the way leads to lower student loans and bills that you will be responsible for upon graduation. Plus, working your way through college helps pay your personal expenses while you attend school.

No matter what job you are working in, or what program you are working for, keep in mind the following tips while you work.

- Be on time for work.

- Do not leave early or take long lunches, unless approved by your supervisor.

- Do not bad-mouth others that you work with. The grapevine leaves a nasty trail.

- Accept constructive criticism rather than getting angry about it.

- Ask for feedback, especially if you do not receive a formal review.

- Be a team player.

- Always put your best foot forward.

7

The Scholarship Jungle

Wikipedia defines a scholarship as:

"A scholarship is an award of access to an institution, or a financial aid award for an individual student scholar, for the purpose of furthering their education. Scholarships are awarded based on a range of criteria which usually reflect the values and purposes of the donor or founder of the award."

Scholarships are another form of "free money" for school. That is why it is in your best interest to explore what is available and what you might be eligible to receive. But like grants, it takes time and effort to find and apply for scholarships.

As with grants, there are different types of scholarships, such as:

- **Merit-based:** Determined by your ability in sports, academics, or other areas

- **Need-based:** Determined by you and your family's financial situation

- **Ethnicity-based:** Determined by your race, religion, or national origin

- **Institutional-based:** Awarded by some colleges or universities

- **Other:** Scholarships are awarded for a number of reasons

When applying for a scholarship, you should remember that:

- You should apply as early as you can — high school is a good time to start.

- The more scholarships that you apply for, the more likely you are to receive one or more.

- Do not assume that because a scholarship is small that it does not count. It all adds up.

- Pay attention to details when filling out all of your forms. Make sure everything is right in terms of content, and that it has no grammatical errors. You do not want to miss a scholarship because you forgot to include something.

- Everyone can find some kind of scholarship they are qualified to receive.

- Keep looking even after you think you have exhausted your possibilities.

- Do not stop at one. You may be eligible to receive more.

During this chapter, you will learn the many ways you can find scholarships, but before we do, let us explore some of the areas where you can find out about college funds from sources you may not have considered before.

- **Try networking for scholarships.** Ask your college friends, your instructors, your relatives, your neighbors, or anyone else who has gone to college or knows someone in college. They may know about a scholarship that you may not have heard of.

- **Do not forget about asking at your school's financial aid office.** While many scholarships are awarded from private sources, your school may be familiar with some of them.

- **Read your local papers**. You would be surprised how often scholarship opportunities are written about.

- **Review bulletin boards and newsletters.** You may spot a scholarship opportunity on your school's bulletin board or even at a local business. College newsletters are also good sources for finding scholarships.

- **Check directly with nonprofit organizations**, such as the Red Cross and the Y.M.C.A., as well as churches, synagogues, and houses of worship.

- **Check with your labor union** if either of your parents work for one. They may have scholarship money.

- **Ask at your local chamber of commerce.** They may be aware of different scholarships offered in your community.

- **Check directly with your college.** Certain colleges have scholarships funds for students who excel but have limited funds.

Defining Yourself

Defining yourself is figuring out how to package yourself best to receive the most scholarship money that you can. You should begin this process as early as possible.

There are some things that you should keep in mind for college even while you are still in high school. These will better prepare you to receive scholarship funds and other opportunities. They include such things as:

- Go to the best high school that you can. If possible, you may want to opt for a private education. If you go to a public school, check the background of the school you are attending to find out its success rate. In some states, such as Florida, the schools are actually graded on test scores and other factors. The best schools receive an A+.

- Even if you cannot choose your school, you generally have a say about what classes you can take. Speak to your guidance counselor as early as you can and see what classes would best help prepare you for your college studies. For instance, if you are headed to a degree in engineering, it makes sense to study higher-level math.

- At some schools you can receive college credit for high school classes by taking Advanced Placement (AP) courses. Again, your guidance counselor should be able to help.

- You might want to start exploring colleges as early as possible just to get an idea of what the college(s) you are interested in expect from new students.

- Think about involving yourself with community services and extracurricular activities. Many schools are looking for well-rounded individuals, and all of this helps to get you into the school you want.

- Start networking now. You may be surprised how early networking leads to later jobs and other opportunities.

- If you have performed community services, or have an excellent status while working part-time in school, it never hurts to start collecting letters of recommendation. That way, the information will be fresh in the minds of those that can write letters for you, and it saves you from backtracking later on.

- If you plan on working during high school, see if you can work in your field or something related. For instance, if you are studying science, perhaps you can get a part-time job in a lab or an animal hospital.

Once you are ready to begin college, you will have a long list of things to do in order to help define yourself and figure out the scholarships that you might be entitled to receive. In Chapter 8, we will cover more specifics on the scholarship process, from writing the essay to filling out your application. However, before that we will explore how to define who you are and how you can position yourself to apply for scholarships effectively.

Some of the items that you will be collecting and working on to help define yourself for a scholarship are listed below. Again, we will cover these in detail in Chapter 8:

- **Letter of recommendation:** Either from a teacher, an alumnus, an employer, a leader in your church, a prominent member or your community, a coach, or anyone else that can point out your strengths.

- **An essay:** This essay by you serves the purpose of convincing admission officers that you should be admitted into their school because of what you have to offer in terms of academic achievements, community service, athletic abilities, and so on.

- **Personal statement:** Often you are asked to write a personal statement that highlights your goals and why you are the best applicant for the scholarship.

When working on defining yourself and figuring out what kinds of scholarships that you might be eligible for, you might want to start with a list of achievements that covers the following:

- **School achievements:** What are school achievements that you can say you have accomplished? Were you in sports? Were you on the debate team? Did you volunteer? What were your grades? Did you work part-time?

- **School contacts:** Who do you know from your school years that could possibly write you a letter of recommendation? Your teacher? Your boss? Your coach? A community leader? A member of your church, synagogue, or place of worship?

- **School degrees/certificates:** Do you have a high school diploma, a two-year degree, a bachelor's degree, or vocational training?

- **Contacts:** Who do you know that can help you get into a school? Do you know anyone that went to a school that you are interested in? Do you know key members of the community? Do you know anyone that holds a political office?

- **Your interests:** What are you interested in? Do you have favorite pastimes? Hobbies? Are you an expert on a subject matter?

- **Memberships:** Are you a member of a club or a community organization?

- **Your strengths:** What are you good at? What would others say that you are good at? Are you a good communicator? Do you have leadership skills?

- **Your focus on studies:** What do you plan on majoring in? What do you plan on minoring in? Are you heading for a bachelor degree, a master's degree, or a Ph.D.?

- **Your focus with a career:** What do you see yourself doing for a living? Do you have a five-year goal with your career? A ten-year goal? For instance, if you are headed for law school, do you want to work for a firm for a few years and then start your own firm?

- **Your paperwork:** Do you have your paperwork in order in terms of your report cards? Social Security cards? Birth certificates? Some of this may be needed for applications to college.

Once you have worked on defining yourself, it is best to keep everything in order. It makes sense to invest in a three-ring binder to hold all of your paperwork. We will review this in detail later in this chapter.

Books

There is a long list of great books out there that are designed to help you find the scholarship money you need. Some books provide a comprehensive list of just about every available scholarship you could imagine. Other books offer helpful tips on filling out the necessary scholarship forms. Some of the books you may find at your local library, others at your local bookstore, still others you can purchase on the Internet.

Let us take a look at a few that you might find most useful for offering advice on scholarships, grants, and other topics, all of which can be purchased at **www.amazon.com**.

- *The Scholarship Book 12th Edition: The Complete Guide to Private-Sector Scholarships, Fellowships, Grants, and Loans for the Undergraduate* (paperback) — An acclaimed guide to private-sector scholarships, grants, and loans.

- *The College Board Scholarship Handbook 2008* (paperback) — Facts about more than 2,100 scholarship, internship, and loan programs offered to undergraduates by foundations, charitable organizations, and state and federal government agencies.

- *The College Board Getting Financial Aid 2008* (paperback) — Gives you the "financial aid picture" for each of more than 3,000 colleges, universities, and technical schools.

- *Kaplan Scholarships 2008: Billions of Dollars in Free Money for College* (paperback) —Features information on programs that offer significant and unrestricted scholarships combined with tips and advice on how to get them.

- *Scholarships, Grants and Prizes 2008 (Peterson's Scholarships, Grants & Prizes)* (paperback) — Provides up-to-date details on millions of privately funded awards valued at billions of dollars.

- *America's Best Value Colleges, 2008 Edition (College*

Admissions Guides) (paperback) — Profiles 150 schools that have low to moderate tuition rates and that are likely to help students by providing financial aid, scholarships, and grants.

- *Get Into Any College: Secrets of Harvard Students (Get Into Any College)* (paperback) — A book of strategy to help you get into the college that you want.

- *US News Ultimate College Guide 2006* (paperback) — Featuring complete data on more than 1,400 colleges and universities.

- *Fiske Guide to Colleges 2008* (paperback) — A leading guide to more than 300 colleges and universities.

- *The Big Book of Colleges 2008* (paperback) — Ranks 201 schools in 20 different categories.

Internet

Besides what you can find out about schools in books, you can also explore Web sites to find out even more, or to supplement your other resources. The Internet is easy to use, plus the information that you find is free.

Before we look at a few great sites, let us cover a few tips for effective Internet scholarship searches and look at what you should watch out for.

- **Use your list:** Gather some of your thoughts from your work on "Defining Yourself" which was covered earlier in this chapter. Use those character descriptions to help you search for a scholarship, such as "high GPA."

- **Be specific:** When doing an Internet search it can be more effective to enter a few words on the search bar rather than just one. For instance, if you are searching for a scholarship for biology majors, type "biology majors scholarships." Be specific in your search.

- **Use different search engines:** While many people use Google, there are other search engines that may provide you with different results, such as Yahoo! and Dogpile.

- **Advanced searches:** Some search engines, such as Google, offer advanced search preferences, which you may want to check out. (They are usually located next to the search bar.)

- **Watch out for scams:** Be careful with application fees or requests for personal information. Just because something is on the Internet does not mean it is legitimate. Watch out for identity theft and financial theft.

- **Do not use paid services:** Why pay for a search when you can find the information yourself? Often, paid searches are not legit. You may be paying for information that you can easily find elsewhere, not "insider information."

- **Make sure they are legit:** Some sites say they "guarantee" scholarships, but that is not realistic.

Some sites have only an e-mail address and no phone number. That should concern you. A legitimate business would most likely offer a phone number as well as a Web site address and e-mail.

According to the Federal Trade Commission, you should be on the alert for scholarship scams:

The FTC cautions students to look for tell-tale lines:

- "The scholarship is guaranteed or your money back."

- "You cannot get this information anywhere else."

- "I just need your credit card or bank account number to hold this scholarship."

- "We will do all the work."

- "The scholarship will cost some money."

- "You have been selected by a 'national foundation' to receive a scholarship" or "You are a finalist" in a contest you never entered.

On their Web site, **www.ftc.gov/scholarshipscams**, the FTC also offers a booklet that you can download: "OUCH... Students Getting Stung Trying to Find $$$ for College."

According to FinAid, the scams are vast and costly:

"Every year, several hundred thousand students and parents are defrauded by scholarship scams. The victims of these scams lose more than $100 million annually. Scam operations often imitate legitimate government agencies, grant-giving foundations, education lenders, and scholarship matching services, using official-sounding names containing words like 'National,' 'Federal,' 'Foundation,' or 'Administration.'"

Finaid.org offers helpful information about scholarship scams and what to watch out for at **www.finaid.org/scholarships/scams.phtml**. The topics cover:

- Common scholarship scams

- Protecting yourself from scholarship scams

- Evaluating scholarship matching services

- Evaluating financial aid consultants

- How to report scams

- Consumer education materials

- How to investigate suspicious offers

- The College Scholarship Fraud Prevention Act of 2000

Now let us review a few helpful sites for finding scholarships. Although there are more sites out there, with this list you should be able to access most private scholarships.

- **www.brokescholar.com** — Access to a database of over 650,000 scholarships worth $2.5 billion in a less-commercial environment than other scholarship search engines.

- **www.Clubscholarship.com** — Over 500,000 awards in a searchable database that allows users to browse for the best matches.

- **www.CollegeAnswer.com** — Gain access to an award database that contains more than 2.8 million scholarships worth over 16 billion dollars, and is expanded and updated daily.

- **www.careersandcolleges.com** — Search over seven billion dollars' worth of scholarships and grants.

- **www.collegeboard.com** — Scholarship Search will find potential opportunities from a database of more than 2,300 sources of college funding, totaling nearly $3 billion in available aid.

- **www.collegenet.com** — Looks for scholarships that match your personal profile or keywords.

- **www.Collegescholarships.com** — Scholarships are grouped by interest, and include middle school and high school awards.

- **www.collegeview.com** — Has been helping parents and students find scholarships and free money for college since 2001.

- **www.ed.gov** — Scholarships are searched by category, such as music and sports, as well as other personal information.

- **www.fastweb.com** — Personalized matching of scholarships to your unique profile.

- **www.internationalscholarships.com** — A resource for financial aid, college scholarships, and international scholarships for students wishing to study abroad.

- **http://aid.military.com/scholarship/search-for-scholarships.do** — Find millions of dollars in scholarships and grants exclusively for the military community.

- **www.salliemaefund.org** — During the 2007–2008 academic year, $2.5 million in need-based college scholarships were awarded to more then 1,000 students nationwide.

- **http://scholarships.fatomei.com** — Competitive and prestigious scholarships, fellowship and internship awards for college study, graduate school, and postgraduate research.

- **www.scholarships101.com** — Access to 800,000 individual awards with over $2.8 billion in scholarships.

- **www.studentawards.com**—Thousands of bursaries, scholarships, and cash awards.

Colleges

While there are private scholarships awarded from various sources, some colleges and universities award scholarships directly to students with high GPAs and low income, or students that excel at sports, or for other reasons. You should always check at the school you are interested in attending to see if they have any direct scholarships that you can apply to receive. Some schools offer search engines directly on their sites for other scholarships as well. More and more scholarships are being added all the time; for instance, Harvard University provided $90 million in scholarships for undergraduate students during the 2006-2007 academic year.

According to their Web site at **www.harvard.edu**:

Harvard Financial Aid Outpaces Tuition Increases

Cambridge, Mass. - March 24, 2006 - Harvard College has announced that it will provide $90 million in scholarships for undergraduate students during the 2006-2007 academic year, eclipsing last year's record-breaking allotment by 6.2 percent. The average total student aid package will be close to $33,000, more than 70 percent of the total cost of attendance. This increase in financial aid support outpaces a 4.75 percent increase in tuition and fees for next year.

Over the past six years, need-based scholarship aid for undergraduates at Harvard has increased by 65 percent while the median graduating debt for those students who borrow has decreased by close to 61 percent to just $6,400 for the Class of 2005, less than one third of the national average graduating debt of nearly $20,000. Two thirds of Harvard's undergraduates receive some form of financial aid, including scholarships, loans, and jobs.

General information about Harvard: 617-495-1000.

Let us look at a few of the scholarships that you can receive nationwide. Keep in mind that each school offers many more scholarships than what is shown below, so check the Web sites for more.

The University of Minnesota

The University of Minnesota offers, among many other scholarships, the Maroon and Gold Leadership Award of $12,000 per year for 4 years. To be eligible, you must be a Minnesota resident and be in the top 5 percent of your graduating class. You must have outstanding academic performance, demonstrated leadership, creativity, community involvement, and contribution to diversity. You may find out about other scholarships offered and apply online at: **http://admissions.tc.umn.edu/ costsaid/schol_campus.html**, or contact:

> **University of Minnesota**
> **Office of Admissions**
> **240 Williamson Hall**
> **231 Pillsbury Drive S.E.**
> **Minneapolis, MN 55455-0213**
> **612-625-5000**

New York University

New York University offers the Helene Fuld Scholarships for entering freshmen. Students with an exceptional background in the sciences are eligible for a $10,000 annual scholarship renewable for all four years of study in the College of Nursing.

The selection process is highly competitive, and only five students are selected each academic year. You may find out more and apply online at: **www.admissions.nyu.edu/financial.aid/scholarships**, or contact:

> **New York University**
> **Undergraduate Admissions Processing Center**
> **22 Washington Square North**
> **New York, NY 10011**
> **212-998-4500**

UC San Diego

UC San Diego offers the Darcy and Robert Bingham Endowed Scholarship that is awarded to current full-time students in good academic standing, employed by UCSD Recreation, UCSD Student Affairs, or UCSD, who work an average of ten hours per week during the three-quarter academic year, and who have worked at least one quarter prior to submitting the application. The award is restricted (based on academic merit plus additional criteria), and is a one-year award of up to $1,500. You may find out more at: **www.ucsd.edu**, or contact:

> **University of California, San Diego**
> **9500 Gilman Dr.**
> **La Jolla, CA 92093**
> **858-534-2230**

Boston College

At Boston College's Lynch School of Education, The Alumni Assistantship Award is available. Established through the generosity of Lynch School alumni, it is comprised of a stipend of approximately $12,000 and a significant tuition scholarship for a student who shows promise of leadership in the field of education or applied psychology. It is given by nomination of the faculty at the time of admission.

The Peter Jay Sharp Urban Scholars Award is also available at Boston College.

The Peter Jay Sharp Foundation has given the Lynch School a generous endowment to provide financial support to ten highly talented graduate students per year who are from underrepresented groups committed to teaching in urban schools. The scholarship is comprised of a $10,000 stipend. One-half of the Sharp stipend is an outright grant, and the remaining $5000 is a forgivable loan. One-quarter of the loan amount will be forgiven upon completion of the master's degree and the remaining three-quarters are forgiven, up to the full amount, for each year spent teaching in an urban school. Tuition scholarships are sometimes paired with the stipend. By nomination of the faculty at the time of admission.

For more information, visit **http://www.bc.edu/ugadmi** or contact:

Boston College
Office of Undergraduate Admission
Devlin Hall 208
140 Commonwealth Avenue
Chestnut Hill, MA 02467-3809
617-552-3100 or (800) 360-2522

Local Organizations

We have examined some of the scholarships you can find from private sources and from the schools themselves, but there are still other places to hunt for "free money" for college. Local organizations, such as the Rotary club, the Kiwanis, VFW, Lion's Club, Retired Teachers funds, and other local groups and organizations sometimes have college scholarships available. Why? The local organizations and clubs make scholarships part of their commitment to serve their communities.

So how do you go about finding these scholarships? Many of these scholarships are posted as announcements in local newspapers, either in the form of ads, articles, or classifieds. The announcements provide you with information on how to go about applying, who might be eligible, and the scholarship amount. If you do not see an announcement for a scholarship in the newspaper, you can check the organization's Web site to see if scholarships are listed. For instance, the Rotary Club of Los Angeles offers awards of approximately $166,000 per year to 77 local students to assist them toward degreed studies. According to the Club:

> "There are four types of scholarships for graduating high school seniors — Close Family College Scholarships, Courtland H. and Edna Hurlock Barr College Scholarships, LA5 College Scholarships, and Past Presidents' Technical Education Scholarships.

> "All scholarships are awarded based on academic achievement, financial need, community and school

service, and personal qualities and strengths. A committee of LA5 members makes the final selection. Each college scholarship will be renewed only if the recipient meets the grade point average requirement and remains enrolled as a full-time student with a minimum of 12 units for the coming academic year."

You can find out more about the Rotary Club of Los Angeles scholarships at:

900 Wilshire Blvd. Suite 418
Los Angeles, CA 90017
www.rotaryclubofla.com
213-624-8601

You might not live in a big city like Los Angeles, but even some Rotary clubs in smaller towns offer scholarships. Take, for instance, the Rotary Club of North Colorado Springs. They award need-based scholarships of up to $10,000 to help cover expenses for the first two years of college. Three to four awards are generally awarded per year.

Rotary Club Of North Colorado Springs
P.O. Box 7056
Colorado Springs, CO 80933
www.northcoloradospringsrotary.org

Kiwanis, Lion's Clubs, and the VFW are other great avenues to check for scholarship funds. While the scholarships may not pay your entire way through college — some of the scholarships are as little as $500 — remember the idea is to apply for as many scholarships as you can to get as much funding as you can. Let us take a look at a few other scholarships that are offered by these local organizations throughout the nation. These are meant to give you an idea of what is available. Be sure to check the local organizations in your area, you may find that several of them offer scholarships that can help you shave thousands off your college expenses.

Keep in mind that these are to give you an idea of what is out there; you should always check local organizations in your area.

The Kiwanis Club of Issaquah, Washington offers scholarships to one graduating senior from three local schools. The scholarships are each a $1,000 cash award to be used to further the student's education. According to the club, eligibility requirements include:

- Applicant will have participated in school and community activities that demonstrate outstanding community service.

- Applicant will have demonstrated academic success.

> **Kiwanis Club of Issaquah**
> **P.O. Box 1111**
> **Issaquah, WA 98027**
> **425-392-4016**
> **info@issaquah.kiwanis.org**
> **www.issaquah.kiwanis.org**

Unlike some scholarships, the Kiwanis Club of Issaquah's scholarship is not need-based. Instead, the scholarship considers your community service experience.

Some local organizations sponsor scholarships for students who are attending a certain school, such as this one sponsored by the Lion's Club in Fairbanks, Alaska:

> The Fairbanks Host Lions Club offers $1,000 to students from the Fairbanks North Star Borough who are attending the University of Alaska Fairbanks, and have been employed while attending school.

UAF Advancement Services
4001 Geist Road Suite 6 • P.O. Box 757530
University of Alaska Fairbanks
Fairbanks, AK 99775
907-474-640
www.uaf.edu

The VFW is also a wonderful organization to check for scholarships. They offer two scholarships programs, the Voice of Democracy Scholarship Competition and the Patriot's Pen Essay Contest.

Created in 1947, the Voice of Democracy (VOD) scholarship program is an audio-essay contest for high school students in grades 9-12 that annually provides more than $3 million in scholarships. The first-place winner, who competes with all the first-place VFW Department winners, receives a $30,000 scholarship that is paid directly to the recipient's American university, college, or vocational/technical school.

Patriot's Pen, a youth essay writing contest endorsed by the National Association of Secondary School Principals' contest criteria, is a nationwide competition that gives students in grades 6,7, and 8 the opportunity to write essays expressing their views on democracy. Annually, more than 115,000 students participate in the contest.

Contestants write a 300-400 word essay based on an annual patriotic theme. The first-place winner receives a $10,000 savings bond and an all-expense-paid trip to Washington D.C. The top national winners each receive a savings bond anywhere from $1,000 to $10,000.

The VFW also awards military scholarships designed to help with education and training. The scholarships provide 25 VFW members with $3,000 scholarships annually. Members must be currently serving in uniform or have been discharged within the 36 months before the December 31 deadline. The VFW also offers the Scout of the Year Scholarship program that provides a $5,000 award to an outstanding scout. Scouts must be recipient of a Boy Scout Eagle Award, a Venture Scouting Silver Award, or a Sea Scout Quartermaster Award.

To find out about eligibility requirements and how to apply, contact:

VFW
General Info 816-756-3390
info@vfw.org
www.vfw.org

The Retired Teachers are nonprofit organizations that look out for the interests of teachers, as well as making a mark in the community with volunteer services and other community work. Some of the associations offer scholarships to the students in the community. You need to check your state's Retired Teachers Association to see if there are scholarships available. Most offer scholarships specifically to those studying teaching.

Contact information varies by state; however, the AARP offers a list of state RTA Web sites at: **http://www.aarp. org/about_aarp/nrta/ed_associations**.

Let us take a look at an example of a scholarship offered by an RTA:

The California Retired Teachers Association offers the Laura E. Settle Foundation. According to the association:

> The program is administered through the financial aid offices of 31 participating University of California and California State University campuses. Scholarships are awarded to students in their junior, senior, or graduate years in an accredited teaching program. The LES Foundation provides $2,000 scholarships to 31 students annually. Another 13 $300 grants from the affiliated Outler fund are also awarded to teachers who plan on working in elementary schools.

> **California Retired Teachers Association**
> **800 Howe Avenue, #370**
> **Sacramento, CA 95825**
> **800-523-2782**
> **916-923-2200**
> **www.calrta.org**

Again, check with you own state's Retired Teachers Association to see if you might be eligible for a scholarship.

Scholarships for Specific Groups

As we have learned previously, scholarship awards are based on multiple reasons, such as need, merit, and those who might be star athletes. However, there are also scholarships created for specific groups, such as minorities and single parents, as well as those that have special interests or are studying a specific field. Many of these scholarships bring diversity to a school or a field of study. For instance, a local engineering group may want to bring more women into the field, so they may offer scholarships for women who are studying engineering. To find scholarships for specific groups, check community service organizations and clubs that pertain to your field of study in your area.

Here are a few scholarships that are examples of special interests and course of studies:

The Vegetarian Resource Group

The Vegetarian Resource Group offers two $5,000 college scholarships. According to the group:

> Due to the generosity of an anonymous donor, the Vegetarian Resource Group each year will award $10,000 in college scholarship money to graduating U.S. high school students who have promoted vegetarianism in their schools and/or communities. Vegetarians do not eat meat, fish, or fowl. Two awards of $5,000 each will be given....
>
> Applicants will be judged on having shown compassion, courage, and a strong commitment to promoting a

peaceful world through a vegetarian diet/lifestyle. Payment will be made to the student's college (U.S.-based only). Winners of the scholarships give permission to release their names to the media. Applications and essays become property of the Vegetarian Resource Group. We may ask finalists for more information.

The Vegetarian Resource Group
P.O. Box 1463, Baltimore, MD 21203
410-366-8343
Email: vrg@vrg.org
www.vrg.org/student/scholar.htm

The NCCPAP / AICPA Scholarships

The National Conference of CPA Practitioners (NCCPAP) and the AICPA have teamed together to offer scholarships to graduating high school seniors planning to pursue careers as certified public accountants. Merit-based scholarships of $1,000 each are awarded.

To apply, the student must be a graduating high school senior with a grade point average of at least 3.3 on a 4.0 scale. The applicant must have applied to or have been accepted at a two- or four-year college and be enrolled as a full-time student. Awards are made for the academic year following application and are sent directly to the school for credit to the account of the student recipient.

NCCPAP/AICPA Scholarships
888-488-5400
Email: lanak.ncCPAp@verizon.net

To look for specific groups scholarships:

- First, make a list of all of your interests and your field of study and search local organizations affiliated with it to see if they offer grants or scholarships. Information is often available on their Web sites.

- Next, check with your school's financial aid office. There may be a scholarships sponsored by alumni groups or in honor of someone affiliated with the school.

- Also search for scholarships on databases, such as **www.fastweb.com** and **www.gocollege.com**. Other potential sources have been listed in this book.

- Do not forget to check local papers. Sometimes the organizations have postings, articles, or ads about their scholarships.

- If there is no Web site for the organization, try making a phone call to them.

- Look at all your options. Search for all available funding. Do not limit yourself in your search.

Keeping Track of It All

When you are applying for scholarships, you may be asked for the same information again and again, so it is best to keep a file with important documents that you might need to fill out your scholarship application. Equally important is keeping track of where you applied and who you applied with. Here are some ideas for keeping track of your important application documents:

- **Purchase a 3-ring binder:** You can use a 3-ring

binder to hold your paperwork and place tabs between the scholarships that you applied for. You can keep copies of all of your important documents in the side folders.

- **Make copies of paperwork:** In the binder, you might want to have the name and address of your school, as well as your own personal contact information, along with letters of recommendations and your essays — which you will learn more about in Chapter 8.

- **Document fees:** If you pay any fees at all, make sure you keep a copy of the check that you submitted. That way you will know how much you sent and when you sent it, in case the check gets lost or misplaced.

- **Write everything down:** Make a note of what scholarships you applied for, the date you applied for each one, what you submitted to each, and where you found out about them, such as what Web site you saw the scholarship on. Again, make a copy of everything you submit.

- **Make a calendar:** Keep a calendar handy to make note of when you applied for each scholarship and when the deadline for applying is.

- **Follow up:** Keep a list of all paperwork that you have to follow-up on and when it needs to be done by. You can also mark the dates for follow up in your calendar.

- **Bookmark pages:** Make sure you bookmark the Web sites that you found the scholarships on. It makes it easier to backtrack.

CASE STUDY: PAUL HOLSTEIN

LifeOrganizers.com

5610 NW 12th Ave, #214

Fort Lauderdale, FL 33309

Phone: (954) 861-6349

Email: info@lifeorganizers.com

www.Lifeorganizers.com

Paul Holstein, Founder of Lifeorganizers.com, and cofounder and Vice President of **CableOrganizer.com.**

I have found that life is best when it's organized, so I created **Lifeorganizers.com**; a growing collection of resources for managing time, home, family, career, and finances, along with a segment dedicated to college students.

HOW TO OVERCOME COLLEGE CLUTTER CRISIS. My personal motto is " HANDLE IT, FILE IT, DELEGATE IT, OR THROW IT AWAY." An easy technique to help you deal with paper and desk clutter is to "handle it" by dealing with it now rather than letting it accumulate and morph into a pile of clutter on your desk. Whatever comes through your inbox, e-mail, mail box, voice mail, cell phone text messages, and even items in your wallet — handle it first by opening it and deciding on what needs to be done with the item. Either you will find a place for it by filing it for reference later, delegate it to the relevant party, or throw it away.

CHOOSE THE BEST FILING SYSTEM FOR YOU. Every piece of paper should have a place where it can be filed out of sight and found easily when needed. A few filing solutions that fit perfectly into small spaces, and dorm rooms, are: a two-drawer filing cabinet, accordion file folders, notebooks with built-in filing pockets; plastic file boxes work great too because they are available in a range of colors and patterns which are not only portable but can be stashed under your bed when not in use. Choose a system that lets you be flexible. You can file according to date, semester, courses, alphabetically or you can even divide your drawer into two sections, one marked as "reference" for papers needed rarely, and the second as a "projects/course work" section for documents referred to most often. Do not forget to make a "finance and budget" section with folders to store your receipts and bills either by month or by the type of purchase.

EMAIL CLUTTER. Keeping like e-mails together will save you endless frustration for when you need to access information quickly. Create folders in your e-mail application to store e-mails by theme or subject. You can have a social folder to keep track of your friends and activities and a course work folder to store lecture notes or class venue changes.

CASE STUDY: PAUL HOLSTEIN

Outlook and most major e-mail applications let you create folders and "rules" to route e-mails directly into their predestined folders according to your preferences.

CABLE CLUTTER. You likely use your computer for college, social networking, downloading music, charging your cell phone and gaming and more, resulting in a lot of peripheral wires cluttering your workspace. There are a variety of products that can help ensure that the cables behind your PC do not become a trip hazard or dust collector. Try bundling your cables using cable ties or shortening their lengths using cable turtles. You may also want to hide them using braided sleeving or make them safer for foot traffic using cord covers. Find out more at **www.CableOrganizer.com**.

Wrapping It Up

Getting a scholarship may take some time and effort. Keep in mind that you should start planning early and apply early for scholarships. You should also apply for as many scholarships that you qualify for. There are plenty of places to look for scholarships; do not just look at one Web site or in one book. Also, do not limit yourself with the types of scholarships that you think you are eligible to receive. For instance, do not assume that just because you are a minority that you should only look at minority scholarships. Keep your options open. Make sure that you keep your scholarship paperwork orderly as you may be using the same information for other applications. Be sure to make copies and keep track of everything you send in and when everything is due. You do not want to miss a deadline when it comes to your applications. Remember that although it takes some effort and time to garner a scholarship, it is that much less you will have to take out in student loans. Once you start making student loan payments, you will be glad you owe that much less every single time you write out the monthly check.

8

Bringing It Home

*L*ast chapter explored the types of scholarships that are available and where to find them. We will now concentrate on how to win those scholarships. There are specific things you can do to increase the likelihood of receiving a scholarship, from filling out your application correctly, to writing a winning essay, to making sure your transcripts are in order, to successfully making it through an interview. By making sure you do it all the right way, you will increase the odds of winning a scholarship and "bring the money home."

How to Win the Dream Scholarship

Like pursuing any of your dreams, it takes time, effort, and planning to win a dream scholarship. "Free money" does not fall out of the sky; you need to work for it and do the right things that will increase the odds of getting it. So where do you start?

- **Keep your information in a safe spot.** Once you have thoroughly researched the many scholarships that you can apply for, gather the necessary paperwork that is needed to complete them. Keep it all in a safe spot. Chapter 7 offers helpful tips on keeping track of it all.

- **Know your deadlines.** Make sure you know the deadlines and apply for each scholarship as early as you can. There is no sense in sending in your information if the deadline has come and gone.

- **Keep track of fees.** There might be fees involved with photocopies, postage, and application fees, so make sure you keep track of money submitted by photocopying your check. (Read Chapter 9 for what to watch out for in fees — you need to be careful for scams.)

- **Read the fine print.** Before sending in your forms, read all the find print to make sure that you have covered everything.

- **Double-check everything.** Check over your application, essay, or other paperwork for grammatical errors, content errors, and typos before you send it in. Double-check to make sure you have submitted everything.

- **Do not leave spaces blank.** Do not leave anything blank. Instead write N/A or 0.

- **Make sure you sign the form**, if it is requested.

- **Only include what is requested.** Do not send in what was not requested, such as a resume.

- **Look for scholarships every year.** There may be new ones available.

Now that we have covered a few of the basics, we will go over what might be requested for your scholarship and how to make sure you have covered everything effectively.

Recommendations

Often scholarship applications require letters of recommendations. And if they do not, it is a good idea to have a few in your pocket anyway, as you may never know when you will need one — from college entrance to job recommendations, references come in handy. You may need three to four letters of recommendation from different sources just for one scholarship application.

A letter of academic recommendation is most effective when it includes specific information:

- The letter should be written on letterhead. For instance, if your boss is writing the letter, it should be written on the company's stationary with the name of the company and the address shown.

- The letter should include background information about who is writing the letter. Are they your boss? Coworker? The letter needs to state their background and their relationship to you.

- The letter should include the title of the person who is writing the letter. Are they president of a company? Instructor from a school? Make sure they sign the document with their title below their signature.

- The content of the letter should also:

  - Contain information about how long the person has known you and in what capacity

  - Provide testimony to your aptitude, attitude, and industriousness

  - Compliment your character, praise your leadership skills, and make mention of your team player approach

- If the letter is a character reference, generally written by family or friends, then the letter can include the following:

  - Stories of hard-work efforts that you made

  - Mentions of your accomplishments

  - Information about memberships or organizations that you belong to and what you have done for the organization

  - Discussion about your personal attributes and strengths

If you are wondering whom you should ask for a letter of recommendation, here are a few ideas:

- Someone who is experienced with your work or efforts

- Someone who can articulately compose a letter

- Someone who has a high title, such as a president of a company

- Someone who would not hesitate to write you a letter of recommendation

A few ideas for sources of letters are:

- Your employer, or immediate supervisor

- A coworker that holds a higher position

- Your coach, especially if you are applying for sports scholarships

- The principal of your school

- The head of an organization that you volunteered your time with

While it is sometimes a little unnerving to ask someone to write a letter of recommendation for you, there are a few ways that you can make the process easier.

- **Timing is important.** Make sure you ask at a good time. For instance, do not ask your boss to write a letter or recommendation when there is a pile of work to do and it is 30 minutes to closing.

- **Explain why you want the letter.** What is the letter's purpose? To get into school? For a scholarship?

- **Be specific about what you need** in the letter and when you need it by. Give them a due date.

- **Supply the letter writer with information** about whom the letter should be addressed to.

- **You might want to explain to the person writing what the letter should cove**r, such as work habits, length of time that you were employed, and so on. Have the information ready for them.

- **You may offer to outline a letter** for the person in order to make it easier for them.

- **Give them a little notice to write it.** Nobody likes having to do something at the last minute.

- **Try to make the process as easy as you can** for the person writing the letter.

Do not forget to:

- Double-check the letter for typos

- Make sure it is signed

- Make sure it addresses what needs to be addressed

- Make yourself a few copies

- Make sure you enclose it with your other scholarship application materials

- Thank the person for writing the letter

The Essay

Of course many scholarships ask for more than just letters of recommendation; some ask that you write an essay, others want to interview you as well — both of which we will explore in this chapter. Essays allow you to show off your grammatical and writing skills, as well as allow you to show off your point of view and how well you can persuade or argue a point. Writing an excellent scholarship essays very important to getting the scholarship, so we will cover this in detail.

When writing an essay, consider the following:

- **Read the directions.** It is vital that you read the directions carefully to make sure you know what your essay is expected to cover. You might want to read the directions twice, just to make sure you understand what is expected of you.

- **Make sure your essay is the right length.** Often the directions will give you a word count. Make sure you do not go over the word count, or under it to any large degree.

- **Meet the deadline.** Do not miss the deadline or you will miss the scholarship opportunity.

- **Organize your thoughts.** Write an introduction to what you want to say, write the contents, and include a summary of what you said. Essays need to be organized and easy to follow.

- **Look it over.** Has your essay addressed what is in

the directions? Does your essay flow? Is your essay easy to read? Does it make sense?

- **Make it interesting.** You want to write something that others want to read. This is no time to be dull! Think of an interesting and compelling topic and how it applies to your experience and field of study.

- **Keep it focused on you**, unless otherwise stated. You are "selling" yourself to the scholarship provider. The essay needs to focus on your strong attributes.

- **Back up what you are saying**. Make sure you are properly referencing your statements. If you are quoting someone, make sure to use proper quotes.

- **Do not steal ideas.** Come up with your own thoughts. This is your chance to shine.

- **Write a rough draft and a final draft.** The more drafts, the better it will be. Do not be too afraid or lazy to rework what you wrote. Good writing takes time and effort.

- **Have someone else look at it.** Get feedback from someone you trust. Ask a writing teacher to look it over. Ask your parents. Ask a friend. Do not assume everything is all right.

- **Double-check it.** Make sure you do not have any typos or grammatical errors.

- **Make sure you have addressed what was asked.** Once you are finished with your essay, go back and read the directions. Ask yourself again if you have covered what was asked.

- **Make copies.** Do not forget to make copies of your essay. Keep your paperwork in a safe place with all of your other materials, as presented in Chapter 7.

- **Mail it**. Make sure you include your essay with your other materials when you send it off. Make sure you do not miss your deadline!

Some scholarships will choose a topic for you. For instance, for a science scholarship, you may be asked to write about something in the science field. However, some scholarships will ask you to choose a topic. If you are choosing your own topic, be sure to pick a good, strong topic that means something to you. You will have a better chance of writing an effective essay if you believe in what you are saying. Also, you might consider writing about something that not only interests you, but also gives insight to the scholarship committee as to what kind of person you are. For instance, if you are applying for a teaching scholarship, you might choose a scholarship topic (if given a choice) on working with students with disabilities. That would give the scholarship committee a feeling that you are concerned with students who may be struggling.

Also, you might want to stay somewhat focused in your thoughts. Keep the angle of your topic narrow, as it will be easier to write something interesting and get into the topic more deeply. Plus, your thoughts will not seemed too scattered.

You can get help with writing your essay on different Web sites. For instance at **www.collegeboard.com**, you can find sample essays, as well as pointers for drafting your own essay and responding to questions. There are also services available to help you write an essay. For instance, Cambridge Essay Service can look over your essay and offer advice for making it better. You can contact them at:

Cambridge Essay Service
617-354-2242
sandy413@yahoo.com
www.hbsguru.com

Or try:

www.essayedge.com

888-GET-AN-EDGE

You can also order a kit to assist you with essays and letters of recommendations:

College Admission Essay Toolkit:
http://instantcollegeadmissionessay.com/ indexmain.html

Instant Recommendation Letter Kit:
http://instantrecommendationletterkit.com/ indexmain.html

There are also plenty of professional writing services available that you can find in your area. You could start by looking at professional resume-writing services. No doubt, they could help you on your essay should you need it. Just make sure that when you send in your essay to the scholarship committee that it is as good as it can be. The potential for scholarship dollars greatly increases with a good, solid, well-written essay.

Filling Out the Application

Along with the essay, you may also be filling out an application. Filling out an application correctly is important for scholarships, grants, and even college entrance and beyond. No matter what the application is for, it is important to fill it out completely. While some applications are filled out online, others are not. Regardless, there are things to keep in mind:

- **Make note of the deadline:** First of all, you should read the deadline for the application. Make sure you still have time to turn it in. Make note of the deadline and get the application in as far in advance as you can.

- **Read the application carefully:** Next, read through the application. Read all of the fine print. Make sure that you meet the eligibility requirements and that you understand what needs to be done.

- **Ask questions if in doubt:** If you have questions, you may want to ask at the source, if possible. Do not make assumptions.

- **Make a copy before you fill it in:** Make a copy of the application and fill out a draft first. You do not want your application to look messy or have something crossed out.

- **Use the right pen:** Make sure you use a black or blue pen to fill out the form.

- **See what is requested:** Find out what other paperwork the application is requesting to go along with it, such as transcripts, a personal statement (see below), or letters of recommendation. Gather them together and do not forget to send them in with the application.

- **Look for fees:** Check to see if there is any kind of fee. If there is, make sure it is enclosed. They may request that you send a money order or cashier's check. If they request that, do not send in a personal check. Read Chapter 9 about scholarship scams to watch out for when sending in any money or personal information.

- **Make a copy of the finished application:** After you have finished filling out your application, be sure to make a copy that you keep on file. Make a copy of the check or money order as well.

- **Keep track of when and where you are sending it:** Make note of when and where you are sending all of your application materials to.

Personal Statement

If your application requires a personal statement — perhaps in addition to an essay or in place of one — it is important to give the scholarship committee a sense of who you are. Follow the directions on the statement request; however, if there are no directions, or if they are general in nature, keep the following in mind:

- Give a sense of who you are.

- State your qualifications for receiving the scholarship.

- State how the scholarship could help you reach your goals.

- State what your long-term academic and career goals are.

A personal statement should always:

- Address what was asked in the directions.

- Be free of typos and grammatical errors.

- Make sense from sentence to sentence and paragraph to paragraph.

- Concentrate on a main topic. Stay on track of what was asked. Do not wander far with your thoughts.

- Make sure your name and contact information appears on each page. That way if the paper gets misplaced or lost, it can be returned to your pile of paperwork.

- Offer a sense of who you are. If you are a leader, then you want the essay to reflect your leadership qualities.

However, every application is different. You may not be asked for a personal statement. If you are, make sure that you follow the guidelines for what the scholarship is requesting for a personal statement. They may ask about your career goals or where the scholarship funds will go. They may want a few words, a few paragraphs, or a few pages. It may be as extensive as an essay or be as simple as a few sentences. Always read and follow the directions closely with each application.

Awards and Achievements

Some scholarships also request information about your awards or achievements. If you have a paper copy, such as a copy of an award that you received for community service work, you might want to send in a copy of the actual award along with mentioning it on the application. Make sure that the application does not say anything about enclosing any extra paperwork; put the application guidelines ahead of everything else. Other achievements you have earned may include things noted in your transcripts. For instance, your GPA will be shown, but it does not hurt to mention a high GPA on your application if there is a place for it.

Keep in mind the following when it comes to awards and achievements:

- Include mention of the awards or achievements that help demonstrate your leadership skills, your willingness to work as a team player, your volunteer work, or other areas that could help shape your character.

- Do not mention something that is not applicable or is missing the mark. If you won an award for "Most Hot Dogs Eaten in 30 Minutes," or something that is irrelevant to your future schooling and career, it should not be included.

- Think about your junior high school years, your high school years, as well as your early college years. You may have awards and achievements that may have slipped your mind.

- If there is a way, try to connect your awards and achievements to how they are a good example for the scholarship. For instance, if you won a leadership award and you are studying business management, perhaps you can tie that into your personal statement somehow.

The Transcripts

As mentioned in Chapter 2, transcripts are required for college application requirements, but transcripts can also be requested by scholarship and grant committees. Transcripts are important, as they contain a record of all courses, grades, and degrees, especially for merit-based work, but they are not all of your application materials. You impress a scholarship committee with more than just your grades; your essay, application, personal statement, and your letter of recommendation all factor in.

Transcripts are sent only at your request, so typically you have to sign a form that says you agree to release them and to where they will be released. A typical fee for transcripts is five dollars per copy of each official transcript that is sent out. Transcripts must be sent directly to the school or organization that is requesting them in order to be official. You can also request a copy for yourself, but they are considered "unofficial." It is a good idea to keep a copy of your transcripts on file for yourself, as you may need a copy to show at your scholarship interview. And it is a good idea to know what they look like.

You can generally request transcripts in several ways:

- By fax

- By mail

- In person

You can often request your transcripts online at your school. Generally, you must fax a signature page back to the school before they are released. If you have several schools to get your transcripts from, it may behoove you to do it all at once. Make a note of when you requested your transcripts. That way, if they do not arrive on time, you can call to find out if they were sent yet or got lost in the mail. There are transcript clearinghouses that you can also use, as was mentioned in Chapter 2, such as the National Student Clearinghouse.

National Student Clearinghouse
13454 Sunrise Valley Drive, Suite 300
Herndon, VA 20171
703-742-4200
www.studentclearinghouse.org.

There are certain circumstances when transcripts will not be sent out, such as if a student has a hold on his or her records.

The Interview

Some scholarships, just like with college entrance requirements, request an interview. We will now examine the interview process and go over what is expected of you and how to make it smoother. Keep the information in mind for other interviews you may have — from job interviews to college entrance interviews — as the process is usually similar for each of these.

Some, but not all, scholarships require an interview. Often, the more competitive the scholarship is, or the more prestigious the school awarding the scholarship is, the more rigorous the process is to getting the money in the first place. That includes an interview. While there are not any concrete ways of conducting an interview, they may be more casual in nature with just a few people in the room, or more extensive with a panel of members waiting their turn to ask you questions. Regardless, a scholarship interview can be intimidating; however, the better prepared you are, the less intimidating they are.

How to prepare before the interview:

- **Bring a copy of the paperwork:** It is best to bring along a copy of all of your scholarship paperwork that was submitted to the scholarship committee, such as your essay, your transcripts, and your application. Just in case something is missing at your interview, you will have a copy in your hand for them to refer to.

- **Review materials:** Review your scholarship

materials before you have an interview. You may be applying for many scholarships and you want to be sure that you are familiar with the one that you are dealing with at the moment. You do not want to get your information confused. Make sure you know what your essay said, what your personal statement covered, and what you wrote down for awards and achievements.

- **Reread the original scholarship application request:** Think about what the scholarship committee might be looking for in a candidate and be prepared.

- **Make notes:** Make notes to yourself about any details that could help you refresh your thoughts. Keep a copy on hand to review the day before the interview.

- **Practice for your interview:** Practice for an interview with family or friends. You could even videotape yourself to see how you spoke and how your body language was during a practice interview. Then go back and redo the practice interview making corrections and improvements.

- **Know the location:** Make sure you know where the interview is. Get your directions ready ahead of time. If you can, you might want to make the drive ahead of time to see exactly where it is and how long it takes you to get there.

- **Figure out where to park:** If the interview paperwork does not state where to park, perhaps you can contact someone at the organization to ask where to park and what the parking fees might be.

- **Bring money to park:** In case there are fees, you want to make sure you can pay.

- **Leave early for the interview:** You do not want any delays or cancellations due to traffic issues or other unforeseen circumstances.

- **Bring contact information with you:** Just in case of an emergency, such as car trouble, you want to be able to call if there is a delay.

- **Get a good night's rest the night before:** It will keep you alert and refreshed.

- **Eat beforehand:** You do not want to think about hunger pangs during your interview or have your stomach growling. Make sure you eat a good meal before you go and bring along a snack, such as a granola bar, just in case you need an energy boost.

- **Wear something professional:** You do not need to go overboard, but dress nice.

- **Arrive early:** Ten to fifteen minutes early is a good amount of time.

During the interview:

- **Do not forget to breathe deeply.** It will relax you, so you can concentrate on your thoughts.

- **Give eye contact to your interviewers.** When

someone is speaking to you, look back at him or her.

- **It never hurts to smile.** Smiling shows off your personality.

- **Sit up straight and watch your body language.** Do not slump or fidget.

- **Listen carefully to the questions** before you answer each.

- **You do not have to rush your answers.** You can take your time to formulate your thoughts.

- **Be honest.** Lying is not going to get you anywhere except on the rejection list.

- **Show pride in your accomplishments.** Do not be pompous and arrogant, but do not hide what you should show off.

- **Ask for clarification if you do not understand something.** It is okay to have the committee rephrase or restate something for you.

- **Do not be afraid to ask questions** about the process, the scholarship, or anything else.

- **Thank the interviewers for their time.** They will appreciate it. If you can, send a note of thanks afterwards.

What might the interviewers ask? It is hard to say exactly what you will be asked during an interview, but hopefully the following will give you an idea of what kinds of questions and topics might be covered so you can be prepare for them.

- You may be asked about your background — from where you were born and raised to what your first job was.

- You may be asked about your school records, your ranking, and what your GPA is.

- You may be asked about what classes you took previously and how they apply to your field of study.

- You may be asked if you have hobbies, pastimes, or do any volunteer work.

- You may be asked about your five-year goals, your ten-year goals, and your lifetime goals.

- You may be asked about your financial picture and how you plan to pay for schooling. Or if you plan on working at all.

- You may be asked about your family and who they are.

- You may be asked about where you plan to reside after college and what job you will be aiming for.

- You may be asked to role-play and answer questions as to what your reaction would be to "such and such," or what you would do in a particular situation.

As you can see, there are very few limits to what you might be asked, but generally the interviewers are trying to get a sense of who you are and where you are headed, and how the scholarship will help you get there.

CASE STUDY: GREG ROLLET

Greg Rollett

Phone: (407) 673-6113

greg.rollett@employmentguide.com

Social Media Specialist at the Orlando Employment Guide

Writer of the Orlando JobSpot http://orlandojobspot.blogspot.com

"So, Tell Me About Yourself."

So your resume got you through the door. Good stuff. Glad to hear it, really.

Now that you are at the door, are you prepared to answer the question that takes most people down before they start? The question that is so relatively simple, yet vague and scary, that it can single-handedly make or break your interview:

"So, Mr. (or Mrs.) Potential Employee, tell me about yourself."

Most interviewees go into the elevator pitch, 30-second sell, or whatever hot term that basically describes yourself in less time than it takes to watch a Super Bowl commercial. This is not a bad route. The problem lies within the context of how you pitch yourself.

Yes, you want to be confident, strong, and truthful. Talk about your career experiences and past employment. Most importantly and probably most overlooked is the fact that you want to sell yourself on the company. How can you help them out? What skills, background, and experience do you have that the employer can utilize to better their organization?

Here are five quick tips to answering the all-important interview question (statement), Tell Me About Yourself:

1. Be honest. They have your resume with contact information right in front of them and they will be calling on your references. Oh, and most employers can call a bluff (it is called counter-questioning).

CASE STUDY: GREG ROLLET

2. Keep it short and relevant. Find your best qualities and skills and limit it to what is important to the company that is interviewing you. There is no need to talk about the process of TV repair when interviewing for a marketing position. Think elevator pitch.

3. Practice. Do not go into the interview blind. More often than not, you have some time between the contact and the first meeting. Practice in front of a mirror, with a friend, or even a family member. (I am sure they want you to succeed and stop mooching out of their fridge.)

4. Research. When talking about yourself, blend in the company's information to show that you have done your part in the research. The Internet poses as a great resource for company information.

5. Eye contact. This keeps both you and the interviewer honest and shows that you want his attention and that he in turn keeps attention to your most important details.

I hope this sheds some light into the all-important first step once you have polished your resume enough to get in the door. Remember, an interview is your chance to really sell yourself both visually and verbally. Keep the focus on the company and be confident in yourself and your skill set and you will be collecting a nice paycheck in no time.

Wrapping It Up

Finding the scholarship in the first place is only half the battle. Once you find it, you may still have a long road ahead of you to get scholarship funds. You might have to fill out a lengthy application, write a personal statement, write a several-page essay, or make it through an interview with a scholarship committee. While it all seems daunting, stressful, and time-consuming, if you break down your scholarship requirements into steps and concentrate on one thing at a time, it is not so bad. Getting "free money" does take time and effort, but in the end, you will be glad you went through the process, especially when you are finished with college and are looking at a stack of student loans to pay. Any scholarship money is that much less that you will owe.

Avoiding Trouble

When it comes to college funding, sometimes it is easy to lose sight of your goal, "Get your degree while going into the least amount of debt." You may try to fool yourself into thinking that you can pay the money back someday, or why should you worry about the money now when you have school to think about, or that you will be making so much money when you graduate, it will be easy to pay back your loans. All of this thinking is wrong. For one, you need to think about paying money back the day you borrow it. You need to think about whether or not the payments will be so steep that you will not be able to afford rent (yes, it does happen!). You need to be responsible about your borrowing and make sure you are aware of all of your loan terms and agreements. Keep in mind that you may not make a whole lot of money after you graduate from college. Hefty paychecks could take years of working in your career to arrive, if they ever come at all.

According to "The Project on Student Debt: An Initiative of the Institute for College Access & Success," students are going into more and more debt, averaging $21,100, yet their salaries are not keeping up:

- There was an 8 percent increase in average student loan debt of graduating seniors between 2005 and 2006 at campuses reporting data for both years. In comparison, starting salary offers for graduating seniors rose roughly 4 percent in the same period.

- The average debt of the class of 2006 reported by institutions — $19,646 — is likely about $1,500 lower than the actual average, due to the limited number of campuses reporting, and deficiencies in the information available to college officials. This means that actual student debt levels are now roughly $21,100.

If you are wondering what your occupation pays, the U.S. Department of Labor Bureau of Labor Statistics offers wages that are defined by occupation and area. Although the site doe not include starting salaries, it does give you a sense of what you will earn in your occupation. You can find out more at: **www.bls.gov**.

The Credit Card Trap

Those little plastic cards look so innocent, but they can sure get you in a lot of trouble. It is easy to forget that all that credit card spending has to be paid back with interest. And interest adds up fast! You could wind up paying twice as much for your purchase if you have a credit card with high interest that you do not pay off every month. Plus, add in late fees, overlimit fees, and you could pay three times as much for the item as it cost in the first place. Let us take a look at the credit card trap in greater detail.

College students are not the only ones who use credit cards a little too much. Most of America uses them on a regular basis, but it sure ends up costing them plenty.

According to CardTrak — the nation's most established and most trusted credit card advisory service for consumers, credit card debt is indeed high:

> PORT CHARLOTTE, FL (May 31, 2007) According to a new survey released today by CardTrak.com, the median amount of credit card debt carried by Americans is about $6,600 while the mean (or average) credit card debt load is nearly $9,900.
>
> Based on an online poll of slightly more than 55,000 consumers that concluded in April, 61 percent said they carry over debt each month on their credit cards, while 31 percent said they pay off balances monthly and 7 percent stated they have no credit cards.
>
> Of cardholders carrying debt, over 64 percent had balances under $10,000. However, an astonishing 13 percent of the same group said they carry total credit card balances in excess of $25,000.

Why does a credit card wind up costing you so much more than if you would have made your purchase in cash?

- Some credit cards you have to pay to get in the first

place — the fees can be anywhere from $25 to $100 or more. Plus, the credit card company charges that same fee year after year, just so you can use the card.

- Some interest rates reach even higher than 22 percent. You may find low-rate cards, but often the low rate is an introductory rate, so it is short-lived.

- Penalty interest rates are typically 30 percent, up to as much as 40 percent.

- Late fees are often $39 a month. And you do not have 30 days to get your payment in on time.

- Overlimit fees are typically $35. Are you wondering why you are allowed to go over your limit? The credit card companies make money off you doing so.

- Credit card companies can increase your interest rate if you are late with your payments. All of a sudden your interest rate will jump, and if you do not pay close attention, you might not even notice that it did. You should check your statement every month to see if the rate increased. If so, find a new card!

Those are many fees that could really cost you if you do not stay on top of paying your bill on time, staying within your limit, and shopping around for a low-interest card. Credit cards stay in business by charging users these hefty fees.

So what do you do if you have racked up your credit cards?

- **Stop using them in the first place.** You are probably spending way more than you need to. When you use a credit card you are paying way too much for your purchase in the long run, once you add up the interest and the potential fees.

- **Try to pay off the entire amount every month.**

- **Do not have many credit cards.** Most of us do need one to make purchases on the Internet, or to place a purchase on hold, but one or two should suffice.

- **Pay more than the minimum payment.** If you cannot pay the entire amount, pay more than the minimum payment; you will save on interest in the long run.

- **Do not be late with your payments.** Credit card companies often do not give you a full 30 days to make you payment. They give you less. As soon as you get the bill, check the payment due date. Make sure you mail in the payment 7-10 days ahead of the due date, so it arrives in time. Better yet, you may want to make your payment online.

- **Ask for help from your credit card company.** If you owe a lot of money on credit cards and cannot seem to make even your minimum payments, try to ask your credit card company for help. They may work with you and give you a lower interest rate, or reduce your payment. You can also request that the due date is changed if it is hard to pay at the time of month that you receive your bill. For instance, if your payment due date is due on the 5th of the month, you can ask that it be changed to the 15th of the month if that is easier for you.

- **Try transferring your balance to a lower-interest credit card.** Some cards offer low rates, even 6-7 percent, for a certain amount of time. It may make sense to find a new card again when the introductory rate runs out.

- **See about home equity.** If you have home equity, it sometimes makes sense to take out a loan to pay off the credit card debt. Your interest will be less and you can deduct the interest paid on your taxes. Check with your tax advisor for details.

- **Get debt counseling.** You might also seek help for debt through American Consumer Credit Counseling. According to their Web site, they are "a non-profit (501)(c)(3) organization, offering confidential credit counseling and financial education to consumers nationwide. ACCC is dedicated to helping people regain control of their finances and plan for a debt-free future." The service can assist you with everything from helping you lower your monthly payment, to reducing finance charges, to reducing or eliminating late fees and overlimit fees.

American Consumer Credit Counseling (ACCC)
800-769-3571
Client Service Department: ext. 500
Counseling Center: ext. 506
www.consumercredit.com

Loan Consolidation Pitfalls

While loan consolidation sounds like a great idea because you lower your payments and interest, it has its drawbacks. But first let us examine why loan consolidation is sometimes the right choice to make before we go into the pitfalls of consolidating your loan.

As mentioned, you typically get a lower interest rate on a consolidation loan than you do with your credit card debt. Consider that credit cards range from 13-30 percent, unless you are able to secure a lower-interest card. The minimum monthly payment is about 4 percent, although each credit card differs. Consolidation may make sense if you can lower the interest rate.

Chapter 5 presented home equity alternatives, which you may want to consider for loan consolidation. Check with a financial advisor before making any decisions about taking out a home equity loan or line of credit, as home equity loans and lines have drawbacks as well.

Let us take a look at a few of the benefits of loan consolidation:

- You lower your interest and payments.

- You can lock into a lower interest rate.

- You only make one payment instead of making several to different credit card companies.

- It is easier to keep track of having just one loan, so you are less likely to be late with a payment.

- You will have a better chance of keeping on top of your payments and avoiding default on your loan.

If you have only student loans that you owe, you might think about consolidating them with a FFEL loan.

According to the U.S. Department of Education:

> A FFEL Consolidation Loan is designed to help student and parent borrowers consolidate several types of federal student loans with various repayment schedules into one loan. With a FFEL Consolidation Loan, you will make only one payment a month. Under this program, your consolidation loan will be made by a commercial lender, credit bureaus will be notified that your account has a zero balance, and you will sign a new promissory note that will establish a new interest rate and repayment schedule. To receive a FFEL Consolidation Loan, you must be in repayment on your defaulted loan (that is, three voluntary, on-time, full monthly payments). Depending on the balance due, the repayment period may extend up to 30 years. If you owe no other delinquent or defaulted debts to the United States, you will again be eligible for other federal funds, including FHA loans, VA loans, and Title IV student financial aid funds.

For more information, and to apply online for loan consolidation, visit: **www.loanconsolidation.ed.gov**.

For a complete list of the federal student loans that can be consolidated, contact:

- The Direct Loan Origination Center's Consolidation

Department, if you are applying for a Direct Consolidation Loan. You can reach them by calling 800-557-7392. TTY users may call 800-557-7395. Or visit **www.loanconsolidation.ed.gov**.

- A participating FFEL lender, if you are applying for a FFEL Consolidation Loan. If you do not know who your FFEL lender is, call 800-433-3243 for assistance.

But before you rush out to consolidate your debt, you need to look at the whole picture, including the drawbacks.

- Debt consolidation can stretch out your loan terms, and even if you are paying less interest, you may pay more in the long run by stretching out the terms.

- Your interest rate or ability to get a loan may depend on how good your credit is. Most lenders are not going to give you an unsecured loan if your credit score is not excellent. Or they give you a less than stellar interest rate.

- You need to be careful about which loans you consolidate. There is no sense in consolidating lower interest loans, such as with some student loans, with higher interest loans.

Additionally, there are unscrupulous lenders out there who are very eager to consolidate your loan, hoping that you will not read the fine print. These lenders charge enormous fees for initiating the loan, ridiculous late fees, and early loan payoff fees, so you have to be very careful about who you borrow the money from in the first place. It is best to start looking for loan consolidation with your bank and see what they can offer you. Also ask your school's financial aid office if they know of a good private source for loan consolidation. Even if you do not wind up taking out your loan with your bank, or with a lender that your school has recommended, you will have a basic starting point to shop around for other loan consolidations. But be on the alert and play it safe.

Some questions to ask about loan consolidation:

- What is the interest rate?

- Is it fixed or variable? If it is variable, how high can it go?

- What is the total amount of all of the loan fees?

- What are those fees for?

- How much are the payments?

- When do the payments start?

- Are there discounts available for making payments online or automatic payment withdrawals?

- Can payments be deferred or reduced? If so, what are the circumstances for doing so? How do you make a request for that?

- Is there a penalty for paying off the loan early? How much is it?

Before making a decision about your student loan you might want to speak with a financial advisor first.

Scholarship and Aid Scams

In Chapter 7 we touched on the topic of scholarship scams, but since it is such an enormous issue, and expensive for consumers, it is worthwhile to spend some time going over possible scams in more detail.

There are plenty of ways to scam people out of anything, and there is no exception when it comes to scholarships, grants, and loan companies looking for a way to bilk you out of your money or your personal information.

Here are a few things to keep in mind when applying for any type of college funding or loans.

- **Do not give money away to get money.** You should not have to pay someone to find you free money. It is not free money if you have to pay someone to get it for you. Besides, you can do you own research for finding scholarships, grants, and loans for free.

- **There are no guarantees.** No one can guarantee that you will receive a grant, loan, or scholarship.

- **Be careful about giving out your identity and personal information.** Unless you are working with a reputable source such as **www.fafsa.ed.gov**, be leery of giving out your personal information, such as your social security number or bank and credit card information. Identity theft occurs often.

- **Watch out for tactics.** "Hurry" or "rush" are scare tactics to try to get you to cave in and act now. Do not trust anyone who uses these measures.

- **Read all documents carefully.** Do not forget to read the fine print. That is where the tricks are often buried.

- **Make sure that you are dealing with a legitimate business.** If you have doubts, do research. Call the Better Business Bureau. Listen to your hunches. If it sounds too good to be true, it probably is.

To contact the Better Business Bureau:

> **The Council of Better Business Bureaus**
> **4200 Wilson Blvd, Suite 800**
> **Arlington, VA 22203-1838**
> **www.bbb.org**

For more information on what to watch out for with scams, visit the FTC at **www.ftc.gov/scholarshipscams**.

Finaid.com offers helpful information about scholarship scams and what to watch out for at **www.finaid.org/scholarships/scams.phtml**.

Report Financial Aid Fraud

A company charging for financial aid advice is not committing fraud unless it does not deliver what it promises. For more information about financial aid fraud or to report fraud, call the Federal Trade Commission toll free at 877-FTC-HELP or 877-382-4357, or go to **www.ftc.gov/scholarshipscams**.

Report Identity Theft

If you suspect that your student information has been stolen, it is important to act quickly. These offices will help you determine what steps to take depending on your situation:

U.S. Department of Education
Office of Inspector General Hotline
800-MIS-USED (1-800-647-8733)
Federal Trade Commission
877-IDTHEFT (1-877-438-4338)

Scholarship Search Scams

Scholarship search scams are a category of scams. What they do is make you pay to have them conduct searches of scholarships that you can conduct yourself for free. And the price can be high.

According to the FTC, "scam artists guarantee 'free money for college' in campus newspapers, flyers, post cards, and on the Internet, and charge from $10 to $400 for their services. According to the FTC, however, students who rely on a fraudulent search service instead of doing their own homework when applying for scholarships or grants will face the upcoming school year bills with nothing for the effort but a hard-earned lesson."

While charging for these services is not illegal, all they are doing is providing you with information that you can obtain for free from reputable sources. No scholarship search company is privy to information that you cannot find out on your own for free, such as at **www.fastweb.com**. Check the appendix for more resources.

What to watch out from with scholarship search scams:

- **Secret scholarships:** As mentioned above, there are not any scholarships that are secret information. Anyone taking some time and effort to find out about scholarships may do so.

- **Guarantees:** A scholarship search company cannot guarantee that you will get a scholarship even if they find one for you.

- **Forcing you to make purchases:** You should not have to make a purchase to have a shot at winning a scholarship. Neither should you be subject to a plethora of pop-up windows and banners trying to entice you to spend your money.

- **Fake scholarships:** Some scholarships themselves are not even legitimate. They are pretending to be scholarships in the effort to bilk you for money or personal information.

Remember to keep your personal information tightly held. Do not give out your social security number, your banking information, your PIN number, or any other information to any source that is not verified as a legitimate business.

Keep in mind that a legitimate scholarship service will not have a Web site with calls to action such as "Hurry!" or "Act now!" These are just pressure tactics trying to entice you to spend your money or offer your personal information before you have had time to check out the background of who is offering you information.

If you are dealing with a company that you suspect is scamming you, document everything. Get it all in writing, and report the company as soon as possible.

Dropping Courses

Sometimes whether you want to or not, you are faced with having to drop a class. You got too busy with work and other classes, or perhaps you are feeling burned out and you want a break, or you decide that you hate the class that you enrolled in. There are many reasons why students drop classes. Dropping a class may be your best bet in some situations, if you do not think you could pass the class, or you changed your mind on your course of study, provided that is it is early in the semester and you can still get a refund.

It is always in your best interest to know when the last drop/add day for the semester is, or you could wind up with an F or a W (withdrawal). But even if you can get a refund, you may still be at a loss by dropping a class.

Some schools may only give you a partial refund for dropping a class, unless it is in the first week or so. But even then, you may still be stuck with losing money on school fees, books, and other expenses that you invested for the class.

Something else to consider before you fill out that drop slip is that by dropping a class, you may be holding down fewer credits than are allowed in order to receive funding, insurance, or other benefits. For instance, your health insurance or your car insurance may be offering you special rates if you are a full-time student. Drop a class or two and you might lose out on your full-time student discounts.

Also, you need to find out if your grants, loans, or scholarships require that you maintain a certain number of credits per semester. You could potentially lose that money if you drop a class. If you plan to drop a class, you need to find out what the minimum amount of classes that you must carry is. Does being a full-time student mean that you have to carry 12 credits a semester or 15 credits? How does dropping a class affect that?

Also, consider your student housing. Does it require that you hold down a certain number of credits each semester? You do not want to get kicked out of your dorm room for dropping a class.

When thinking about dropping a class you should also consider graduation. Is dropping the class going to throw off your graduation date? Is the class that you are dropping a required class, meaning you will have to take it and get it over with at some point? Is it a prerequisite for other courses, so that dropping it is going to mess up your next few semesters' schedule?

Before you drop a class, find out what financial considerations you should think about, including loans, grants, scholarships, and your housing. Also find out about the feasibility in terms of how this will affect your graduation plans.

If you are having trouble with a class, you could speak with your professor about how to make the class go smoother. Perhaps you can get a pass/fail grade instead of a letter grade, or ask about an incomplete. You could speak with your advisor and find out about tutoring. Some schools offer help with tutoring. You could buckle down and just finish the class. You have some choices and you may find that the best one may be sticking it out and finishing the class.

Dropping Out

It is unfortunate but true that at many colleges many of the students do not finish their degrees.

According to Fastweb.com, "Almost 60 percent of those attending public universities do not complete their degrees within five years—and more than 70 percent of U.S. students earning four-year degrees attend public universities."

Some students cannot handle the academic rigors; some realize that they cannot afford college. Others wind up in life-changing situations so that college is not feasible. No matter what obstacles you come across, however, it is a good idea to try to finish.

Generally, those who earn degrees make more than those without a degree. Plus, if you drop out of school, you may have to pay money that was given to you as a scholarship or grant. (Check your funding source for details.) Not to mention, you will begin paying your student loans much sooner.

As was mentioned in the Preface, according to a 2007

College Board study, education pays: "Over a lifetime, the gap in earning potential between a high school diploma and a B.A. is more than $800,000."

When you think about the cost of dropping out of school, you might want to reconsider trying to find a way to work on your degree.

You could look into night school, online schools, or look at extension classes. You can find plenty of accredited degrees from many schools that offer these alternative means of getting your education. Even at the school you are attending now, you may be able to take some of your classes online, or take them during the evening to free up time for a part-time job. Or you may be able to take some of your classes through extension which is generally quite a bit cheaper than through the regular school program. For instance, at Harvard you can enroll in an extension class for about $550 per lecture course, whereas you would pay about $4,000 per course at Harvard University.

However, do not assume that your grant or scholarship money will transfer with you. It may or may not.

If you are having money troubles, there are things you can do to lift your bank account. For instance, have you applied for all the possible funding that you can receive for college? Have you cut your discretionary expenses? Can you cut your living expenses by getting a roommate or moving back home? Can you get a part-time job? Chapter 10 will offer a few ways to help you cut your expenses.

Before you assume you cannot afford school, consider whether you can really afford to drop. In the long run, it may cost you quite a bit more, considering lost earning potential. For example, what if you were attending college to become a doctor, but wind up dropping out? How much money do you think you might lose in a lifetime by missing out on receiving a doctor's wages year after year?

Before you drop out of school, always speak with your academic advisor. He or she may have some good insights or ideas that can help you figure out a way to make staying in school work.

Wrapping It Up

Just as important to finding great deals and free money for college is staying on top of the money you have and avoiding getting scammed. Keep in mind that if something sounds a little fishy, it probably is. If it sounds too good to be true, that is probably true as well. Keep your eyes open and your wallet and personal information close to you. If you suspect a scam, document everything and make sure you report the scam to officials.

If you are thinking about dropping a class, or dropping out of school, keep in mind what you may run into financially. Dropping a class may cost you your scholarship, your housing, or your insurance. Dropping out of school can cost you a lifetime of lost earnings. Think hard before making decisions about your school. Speak with your advisor about the implications of your school decisions. He or she may have the right advice to help you make the right decision.

Living Cheap

hroughout this book we have focused on how to bring more money into your pockets by applying for grants, scholarships, loans, and more. During this chapter, we will concentrate on ways that you can cut back on your expenses, ranging from where you live, to how you can cut medical expenses, to where you can find deals on books and supplies. Even if you get loads of scholarships and grants, it is still a good idea to cut your expenses down to a minimum. Even with free money for schooling coming in, you would be surprised how fast it goes out the door. And if you think you can cover all the extras with the aid of student loans, remember that keeping your student loans down to a minimum is your best bet. We will explore the many ways you can save on your living expenses and keep the cost of going to school as inexpensive as it can be.

Choosing Where to Live

Where you decide to go to school may make your decision

for you in terms of the area that you will live. However, if you have a few schools that you are interested in attending and they cost about the same amount of money for tuition, you might want to look into the cost of living at the college. If you are staying in a dorm, how much does it cost? What does it include? If you are staying in student housing, what is the rent? If the school is located in a big city, you might have big city expenses that you might not incur if the school is located in a smaller town. Plus, the food and gas may be higher as well. There are different Web sites that can help you find what the cost of living is in the town you are considering. For instance, DataMasters offers surveys where you can find out about the cost of living, along with your expected salary for your field.

DataMasters
www.datamasters.com

Another Web site that provides you with a list of cities or towns that might best fit you is "Find Your Spot." The site has you fill out a short survey of what you want and do not want in a city or town and you are given a few ideas of places that would suit you. This makes some sense to look into while going to college and upon graduation.

Find Your Spot
www.findyourspot.com

Choosing which city might fit your budget better is only part of the equation. If your city is already decided, meaning you are going to a certain university in a certain city, you have choices to make about where you are living. You can choose to live on campus or off. You can choose to have roommates or choose to live alone. You can choose to live within driving distance or walking distance, or you can choose to live on a bus route. You can choose to be in the middle of the action or live in a quieter place. If you are attending school online, you can choose to live anywhere. Where you decide to live is based on your budget, your lifestyle, your personality, and what is important to you.

When trying to make a decision about where to live, you might want to think about the positives and negatives for each situation. For instance, if you are contemplating having a roommate, you may think about the extra money you will save on rent, and the possibility of having company or friendship. The negatives might be that you have to share a space with a person who may be sloppy, loud, or too talkative — especially when you are trying to study. If you are thinking about a dorm room, you may enjoy all the socializing that comes along with it, but the dorm room may have certain rules that you have to abide by, such as curfews. Think about the positives and the negatives for each choice you make, and hopefully you will be able to make the right decision for where to live during college. It really depends on what is right for you.

CASE STUDY: SUSAN JOHNSTON

Susan Johnston, Freelance Writer

SusanEJohnston@gmail.com

http://www.susan-johnston.com

Cheap Dorm Room Decorating Ideas and Tips

Your dorm room will be a home away, so it should be a place where you can study effectively and provide safe sanctuary from outside stress.

Here are a few suggestions for making it comfortable and stylish:

CASE STUDY: SUSAN JOHNSTON

The Basics of Bedding

The bed often doubles as a coffee table, couch, or study area, so it is key to choose a comforter that reflects your style and will not immediately show the dirt. A comforter helps determine the color scheme for the rest of the room, so choose one you like. Reversible, solid-colored comforters are a good choice, because they offer twice as many design options.

Think Storage

Space is tight in most dorms, so maximizing storage is a must. Try raising the bed with cement blocks or RackRisers to make space under the bed. You can also stack plastic crates in your closet, under your bed, or next to your desk. An alternative to plastic crates is a wire storage system, which lets you assemble your own crates and dismantle or reorganize them later. Or use decorative hat boxes in varying sizes. Buy closet organizers for shoes, skirts, accessories, or makeup. Also invest in some cheap plastic hooks, and just stick them to your closet door to hold a bathrobe or jacket. Tables can do double-duty for TVs and computers.

The Wall Is Your Canvas

Always check your school's rules before painting, punching holes, or even using tape on the walls. Some colleges have a poster sale at the beginning of the year where you can snag some highly unusual and inexpensive finds. Poster adhesive, found at decorating stores, can be safely used. Unleash your inner artist and draw a new mural or work of art once a month or whenever you feel inspired by using colored chalk, or butcher paper and colored pencils. Frames are essential for holding photos of home or new friends. French memo boards can hold a whole bunch of pictures, ticket stubs, or magazine cutouts. A laundry line is a great alternative for you to string up pictures or ticket stubs on the wall or across the room. Magnets are useful and decorative on any metal surface. Dry erase boards are handy for communicating with friends and roommates and keeping track of your busy schedule.

Other Thoughts

Sheer fabric draped across the window or over a bed creates a soft, romantic look. If you have an open closet, put up a colorful shower curtain to individualize your space or hide dirty laundry. A desk lamp for late-night studying is a necessity, but adding mini-lights across the room can create a more personal atmosphere. White lights will complement any décor, or choose colored lights in funky shapes like stars, cactuses, or hearts.

To Drive or Not to Drive

When you think about the environment, we should all be walking or riding bikes. While that is not totally possible, it is something to consider doing when you can. Besides offering a clean-air alternative, bike riding keeps you in shape and keeps your stress level lower. If you do not have a bike, you can usually find a good deal on a new one at a sporting goods store, otherwise keep your eyes out for a good used one in the want ads, or online at sites like **www.craigslist.com** or at garage sales. You never know, you may just find a great bike that is hardly used. But you may be living in a location where it is not possible to bike; perhaps it is too cold or you live to far from school, or maybe you are taking night classes and it is unsafe to walk or bike. Can you consider the bus? Buses are also better for the environment, plus, they are a lot cheaper for you to use for transportation — much more than driving a car. Some cities offer bus passes for the month where you pay a flat fee for unlimited rides. For instance, in Los Angeles, monthly LADOT passes start at $40 per month. That is a whole lot less than it costs to drive a car, especially once you consider gas, maintenance, and insurance. Check with your city for details on bus passes.

Los Angeles Department of Transportation
www.ladottransit.com

If you are living in a city such as Chicago, New York, or San Francisco, you can easily get around without a car. You have options such as trains, cabs, and buses that are a cheaper alternative than owning a car.

If you cannot walk, ride a bike, or take the bus, you can save money when using your car by taking several measures:

- **Car pool.** Find fellow students that need rides and get them to chip in for gas. If you do not know anyone that wants to carpool, you can post a notice on a school bulletin board or in the school newspaper.

- **Use a gas credit card.** Some gas credit cards give you money back for purchases. You have to purchase gas anyway, so you might as well get a rebate.

- **Drive a fuel-efficient car.** If you have not bought a car yet, make sure you purchase one that gets good gas mileage. Or better yet, buy a hybrid.

  For better fuel efficiency:

  – Keep your tires well inflated.

  – Change your air filter frequently.

  – Keep your car tuned up.

  – Avoid long idles if you can.

  – Use the air conditioning less.

  – Do not top off your gas.

- **Cut out unnecessary trips.** Think about where you are driving and try to do all your errands while on the trip without backtracking. Figure out the shortest way to get from point A to point B when driving anywhere. Purchasing a GPS may be a good idea.

- **Walk some and drive some.** Perhaps you cannot get away from owning a car, but you can try to walk to some of your locations, or bike sometimes. The gas you can save will really add up.

CASE STUDY: SHEL HOROWITZ

Accurate Writing & More

16 Barstow Lane

Hadley, MA 01035

(413) 586-2388

www.frugalfun.com

Shel Horowitz, Owner and Author

The Most Frugal, Eco-Friendly, and Elegant Transportation Around!

What could be better for the frugal college student than...the humble bicycle?

The bike is one of the most empowering technologies ever invented: a combination weight-loss, fitness, recreation, transportation, and exploration device. It allows you to spend time with loved ones or by yourself, having FUN! Whether you prefer to fly down a hillside at top speed or cruise leisurely through a beautiful park, the bike offers you a chance to do it.

Consider this:

- A bicycle costs almost nothing to operate, and its manufacturing impact is a lot lighter on the earth than a car, motorbike, or moped.

- In crowded urban areas, bikes are often faster than cars on trips up to about 5 miles (roughly 9 km if my math is right), and the majority of car trips are less than that.

- Rural areas with poor public transit are often delightful places to ride: hardly any traffic, clean air, open scenery.

- Even people with certain disabilities can often enjoy a bike ride — on a hand-powered recumbent model, for instance.

CASE STUDY: SHEL HOROWITZ

- There's nothing as good as a bike for getting from one end of campus to the other fast and hassle-free.

- Bike paths, bicycle parking, bike racks on public buses, showers, and other amenities have been installed in many areas — and if your area is behind the times, start asking for what you want!

I started commuting by bicycle as a sophomore in high school, in New York City. My trip was three miles of flat terrain. But when we moved a year later, my ride was 5-1/2 miles uphill. On my three-speed, I still routinely beat the bus, which took a convoluted route.

Later, when I worked in Manhattan, I would bike several miles to a better subway station with a more direct route to work. Even after moving to New England, I still used my bike constantly to get around town. Now, unfortunately, we are in a steep, curvy area along a state highway, and it is much harder. But I still bike to the post office sometimes, or strap the bikes to the car, drive a few miles, and ride along the bike path. Some bus companies are even installing bike racks now. The ability to combine bikes with other modes of transportation provides incredible flexibility.

So, what are you waiting for? Get that old bike out of the garage, pump up the tires, and go for it!

Shel Horowitz is the owner of **http://www.frugalfun.com** and the author of *The Penny-Pinching Hedonist: How to Live Like Royalty With a Peasant's Pocketbook* — a 280-page book on how to have fun cheaply — as well as several business books on frugal and ethical marketing.

Doing Without

Like most Americans you are probably caught up in consumerism. You are buying things you really do not need, or even want, just because you feel like you have to. Thanks to the bombardment of advertising, many of us are caught in the consumerism trap. We end up spending way too much money, more than we make, and more than we need to. So how to stop?

Start off my keeping track of your expenses. Buy a small notebook and start keeping track of where your money is going. You can always use budgeting software, but a notebook is cheaper and works just as well. After a week or so, take a look. You will be surprised to see where the money is going. Some of it is going to fixed expenses, such as rent, gas, insurance, and other expenses that really do not change. Other money is going out to discretionary expenses. Those are expenses that are not set every month. It is where you can really look at cutting back on spending first. But you can always cut back on your fixed expenses by moving to a cheaper apartment, getting cheaper insurance, or even selling your car.

Once you see where the money is going, you can look at ways to reduce. For instance, if you are eating out every single day for every meal at an average price of $8 per meal, that's $720 per month out the door for food. Surely, you do not need to spend that much on food every month. Buy some groceries and make some meals at home, even if it is sandwiches. Sandwiches are just as quick and easy as fast food and probably a whole letter better for your health.

You should also take a look at your impulse purchasing. Stores are set up to offer plenty of impulse purchases right by the register, such as candy bars and magazines, so you ponder buying them while waiting in line, and typically you fall for a purchase. Cut back on those impulses.

Another place to cut back may be with your entertainment. While you may love to go out with your friends, why not try inviting friends to your house instead of meeting them at a local pub? If you love going to the movies, trying renting movies at least some of the time. You do not have to completely change your lifestyle to cut back on spending, but you can alter it some and save money in the process.

When it comes to clothing, try thrift stores or consignment stores. You may find what you need for just a few dollars.

There are plenty of great Web sites out there that offer great ideas for living on less; you should check them out for ideas on how to incorporate some of this into your life — at least until you finish school.

A few good frugal sites:

- **www.thefrugallife.com** — Contains information on how to live frugally with what you have.

- **www.livingonadime.com** — Offers newsletters and articles with money-saving tips.

- **www.zenhabits.net/2007/08/the-cheapskate-guide-50-tips-for-frugal-living** — Offers a forum to help you save on money by cutting back on expenses.

You could also check for free stuff at **www.freecycle.org**. According to Freecycle, "Our mission is to build a worldwide gifting movement that reduces waste, saves precious resources, and eases the burden on our landfills while enabling our members to benefit from the strength of a larger community."

Eating Right

Even if you are a poor college student, it is important to eat healthy. Eating healthy will give you more energy, make you feel better, make your stronger, lower your risk of disease, and keep you living longer. Even if you do not have lots of money, you can still eat healthy.

If you are looking for best bargains at the grocery store, try shopping in the perimeters. The middle aisles are packed full of prepackaged and expensive foods. The healthiest food is found in the outside aisles. Also, when heading to the grocery store, bring along a list of things to buy. You will cut back on impulse purchases which will leave more money to buy healthy foods. If you buy bulk items and split them with a friend or roommate, that will help shave costs too. Also, if you have a food co-op available, you might want to try shopping there before the grocery store. Co-ops are customer-owned business that offer high-quality, fresh, locally grown foods to their members — all at a great value.

You can find local farmers markets by visiting:

- **www.farmersmarket.com**

- **www.ams.usda.gov/farmersmarkets**

Do not forget farmers markets and roadside fruit and vegetable stands. They are often loaded with great deals on local foods. Many veggies can be packed along in your backpack if you get the munchies, such as mini-carrots and cut celery. Frozen veggies also work, as they stay fresh in the freezer and do not go to waste.

Drink plenty of water. If you are looking for the cheapest drink available, look no further than your kitchen faucet. Some city water actually tastes just fine, so even if you drink some bottled water, you can still tap into the tap and save money. Remember that drinking eight glasses of water every day is good for your digestive tract and keeps you hydrated and refreshed.

You do not need meat every meal. Cheap sources of protein can be found in beans, eggs, and whey powders that you can use for shakes. Check at your local health food store for a container of whey powder.

For breads, opt for whole-grain breads and cereals. They may cost a little more, but are much better for you.

A few more tips about saving money on food:

- **Do not forget about generic and store-brand items.** Often the taste is just as good and sometimes better than the name brand, and they are generally quite a bit less.

- **Plan your meals and write down what you need.** That way when you head to the grocery store, you are buying the items you need and not forgetting anything — plus, it saves a trip back to the grocery store and saves on gas.

- **Try to eat less.** Yes, you can save money by cutting back on eating, especially if you are snacking out of boredom or frustration. You not only save money, but you stay in better shape.

- **Do not eat junk food.** It is not good for you, and it is more expensive.

- **Eat out less often.** It is definitely more expensive than eating at home, especially when you add in a tip and gas for getting there.

- **If you can cut coupons, do so.** Only cut out the ones that offer you deals on food you will buy. There is no sense in purchasing items that are on sale, only to let them rot in your cupboard.

A Few Healthy Snack Ideas

- Water. You may not really be hungry, but instead just thirsty. Try water first.

- A can of soup fills you up. Make sure it is low in sodium.

- Microwavable oatmeal. You can enjoy it in many different flavors.

- Dried fruits such as raisins, apricots, or cranberries.

- Crackers or pretzels. Opt for whole grain or whole wheat.

- Nuts and trail mix. You can always make your own trail mix. It is cheaper to make a batch and you can add in just what you want.

- Granola bars. That is if they are low in fat.

- Fresh fruits or veggies. Slice up a few for the week.

CASE STUDY: CHARLI MILLS

Charli Mills, Food Writer

16219 Excelsior Circle

Rosemount, MN 55068

(952) 431-4811

indigomum@msn.com

charlim.gather.com

Organizing a Pantry to Save Time and Money

We live in an era of mega-supermarkets, modern appliances, and fast food. All is designed to be quick, quick, quick. Yet, to the college student living on a shoe string, convenience is expensive.

Organizing a pantry can help you save time, money, and gas. When I was a college student, I had three young children and a household to manage. Money was tight. When my oldest daughter went to college she remembered how we cooked from scratch and organized our shopping. This early influence helped her save money while in college.

A pantry is a place to store food that does not require refrigeration. It can be any kind of storage space. You want to store inexpensive staples in your pantry to extend your food budget and reduce your trips to the grocery store.

To save time, organize according to what you use. Create space for different meals. You can post a corkboard on the inside door of your pantry area to keep track of schedules, menus, and grocery lists. Take time to create a weekly menu so you are less apt to order out or skip a meal. It will also reduce the number of visits to the store. As you run out of staples, note it on your grocery list.

Take advantage of sales and stock up if you can. Be careful not to buy on impulse and avoid prepackaged meals. If possible, buy in bulk. Most staples like grains, pasta, and dried fruit are available in bulk. Use jars as containers, which can be found at most second-hand stores or by reusing jam or peanut butter jars. Bulk is always less expensive than packaged counterparts.

Having a pantry requires a commitment to cooking from scratch, but it is not as difficult

CASE STUDY: CHARLI MILLS

as it sounds. For instance, homemade soups, pasta dishes, and bread are easy enough to learn. Recipes are available online, at stores, and from family members. Cooking can be a group activity with roommates or classmates pitching in and sharing the results. A large crock-pot is an inexpensive investment and makes preparing food easy.

Here is an organized list for a well-stocked pantry:

Breakfast Pantry Staples

- Granola
- Jam
- Cream of Wheat
- Pancake mix

- Cereal
- Oatmeal
- Maple syrup

Lunch Pantry Staples

- Canned tuna
- Bread (homemade)
- Crackers (homemade)

- Peanut butter
- Dried fruit
- Seeds (less expensive than nuts)

Dinner Pantry Staples

- Rice
- Dried beans
- Canned vegetables
- Tomato paste and sauce

- Pasta
- Canned tomatoes
- Canned broth
- Cooking oils and vinegars

Bulk Staples & Spices

- Flour
- Whey
- Cocoa powder
- Baking powder

- Oats
- Sugar
- Baking soda
- Salt

CASE STUDY: CHARLI MILLS	
• Pepper	• Garlic
• Dried onions	• Oregano
• Cumin	• Chili powder
• Parsley	• Any ethnic spices like curry

Raid your parents' pantry when you visit, and keep yours organized and in regular use. For fresh items, consider looking for local dairies or farms that will sell you milk, cheese, eggs, and even beef, chicken, or pork. Carpool to the grocery store, co-op, farmers market, or farm. Master an organized pantry and you will succeed in living on a shoe string.

Medical Expenses

While you cannot always change the fact that you will incur medical expenses, there are ways that you can cut back on your bills.

For instance, if you are taking a prescription, it is best to always ask for the generic version, as it can be substantially less than the name-brand version of the medication. Also, if you are taking an expensive medication, it makes sense to shop around for the best deal. Yes, pharmacies do charge different amounts. Also, you can apply for an activated Rx discount card, which can yield savings of up to 75 percent at more than 54,000 national and regional pharmacies. Learn more at **www.FreeDrugDiscountCard.com**.

If you need to go to the doctor, find out if your school has an on-campus health center, or find a free or low-cost clinic. You can generally get basic healthcare even if you have no insurance. Plus, payment is on a sliding fee scale. At the U.S. Department of Health and Human Services' site, you can find an HRSA-supported health center in most cities and many rural areas. To find one in your area, visit:

**U.S. Department of Health and Human Services
Health Resources and Services Administration
www.ask.hrsa.gov/pc**

According to the U.S. Department of Health and Human Services, health centers provide:

- Checkups when you are well

- Treatment when you are sick

- Complete care when you are pregnant

- Immunizations and well-child care for your children

- Dental care and prescription drugs for your family

For instance, in California, the Venice Family Clinic provides free, quality healthcare to low-income patients who lack private health insurance — from comprehensive primary healthcare, to mental health services, to health education and child development services, along with prescription medicines that are provided at no charge. Their Web site is **www.venicefamilyclinic.org**.

If it is dental care you need, you might try a dental school for basic cleaning and some dental care. The work at the schools is generally performed by students, but is supervised by experienced dentists.

For instance, at the University of Minnesota Dental Clinics, general and specialty dental care in association with the

School of Dentistry's educational programs are provided to more than 100,000 patients per year — all for a fraction of what it would cost to visit a dentist.

University of Minnesota, School of Dentistry
Moos Health Sciences Tower
515 Delaware Street SE
Minneapolis, MN 55455
612-624-8400
www.dentistry.umn.edu

A few tips to save on medical bills and insurance:

- **Double-check your medical bills**. You would not believe how often your bill is wrong, and you do not want to be overpaying.

- **Shop around for health insurance.** Think about a high deductible or even major medical.

- **Look into different co-pays on your insurance.** The higher your co-pay, the less you pay for the monthly premium.

- **Try to negotiate for a self-pay arrangement** with your doctor. They often offer cheaper rates for self-pay.

- **Reduce co-payments;** negotiate prices with your doctors.

Your best medicine is always to take care of your health and your teeth in the first place. You will look better, feel better, and stay healthier for longer.

Here are a few tips for staying healthy:

- **Make sure you get enough sleep.** You need at least eight hours nightly, not four or five. Without enough sleep your body cannot rest and repair itself. Plus, you will be drowsy and perform less effectively.

- **Make sure that you eat a healthy diet.** Your diet should include plenty of fruits and vegetables, whole grains, and proteins every day.

- **Take a multivitamin every day.**

- **Get your exercise.** Try to get at least 30 minutes a day.

- **Do not smoke.** It is not only bad for you, but it is an expensive habit.

- **Keep your stress level down.** While going to college can be stressful, there are ways you can reduce your stress:

  - Breathe deeply

  - Meditate

  - Take long walks

  - Do something you enjoy

  - Enjoy the company of others

  - Talk it over with friends

  - Keep caffeine down to a minimum

Cheap Books

According to National Public Radio, "More than a dozen states are considering laws that would restrict price increases for college textbooks. With many books now costing more than $100, college students and their families are facing huge bills on top of tuition costs."

Why? Because books are a tremendous expense for students to incur on top of all the other expenses, such as tuition, fees, and housing. Some of the instructors have actually written the textbooks, so there is that to consider as well. Plus, every year it seems there is a new edition, driving students to always have to purchase the latest copy and hence doing away with the ability to make purchases of used books. Plus, books often have CD-ROMs that are enclosed with the books, just to drive up the cost even more.

Do we need all those expensive textbooks? Probably not, now that the Internet and eBooks are so available. Hopefully someday some of the demand for buying textbooks for college classes will be limited or eliminated, but until then, we need to make the best of it and get the books as cheaply as possible.

There are various organizations that are working on policies to help lower the cost of textbooks, such as **www.Make TextbooksAffordable.com**. According to them, there are ways you can save on textbooks.

Five Ways to Save on Textbooks Now

- **Buy or rent textbooks online.** There are hundreds

of sites where students can buy, sell, and even rent textbooks for a fraction of the cost. Some basics include **www.amazon.com**, **www.campusbooks. com**, and **www.half.com**. To find other good Web sites, here are some keywords to search: "used textbooks," "[your school] bookswap," "textbook price comparison," or any ISBN.

One potentially interesting new service is Textbookflix, which is modeled off online video rental services like Netflix and Blockbuster. Students choose their required books from an online book list, pay the rental fee or subscription fee, and the company sends the book to the student. At the end of the term, the student simply drops the books in the mail with a prepaid envelope. Although we have not done a full evaluation of Textbookflix, this could be a major money saver for students having a difficult time finding used books.

- **Shop overseas.** Many American textbooks are available at a fraction of their cost here through overseas Web sites. Check out foreign versions of leading American Web sites like **www. amazon.co.uk**, or you can also get overseas prices for Thomson Learning books by going directly to their Web site and clicking another country at the main page. Shipping can often take several weeks, so make sure to leave enough time. Also, foreign editions may have minor differences; so as a rule of thumb make sure the "ISBN" matches.

- **Swap.** There are many ways to find used books to buy, borrow, or trade just by contacting other students:

  - **Ask around:** Ask your friends, your friends' roommates, etc. It is not hard to find someone who has taken the class before, and you will save on shipping too.

  - **Facebook:** Look for used book groups (yes, they exist) and search for people who have taken the class before. Try Craigslist and MySpace also.

  - **Bookswaps:** Use nonprofit student-to-student sites like **www.campusbookswap.org** or your student government's Web site.

- **Check it out.** School libraries often stock copies of commonly used textbooks. If you get there early you might be lucky enough to check one out, but at the very least instructors will typically put one copy on reserve at the library for everyone to access. If you cannot get a book for free, you might still save money by renting. There are several online rental programs that might have the book you need, and several colleges and communities have locally based programs, too (start one at your school).

- **Do your homework.** Ask professors if you can use an older edition or a version without any "bundled" items like CDs. To make the search easier, ask your instructor for the ISBN number, which is the unique code for each book.

Here are a few other good sites to buy and sell used textbooks:

- **www.textbookx.com**

- **www.bigwords.com**

- **www.iCollegeWeb.com**

- International Book Deals at **BestWebBuys.com**

These sites offer long-term solutions for lowering the prices, as well as recent news about what is happening in the legal sector with regard to lowering the cost of textbooks.

So what is so great about buying online?

- It is fast and easy.

- You save money buying used textbooks.

- You can generally find the textbooks you need.

But keep in mind that you will also incur shipping expenses when purchasing online.

The Cost of Going Home

If you are living close to home while attending school, making a trip back home is relatively easy. You fill up your tank, jump in your car, and head out. If you want to save on gas, find out if you can carpool with a fellow student. For others, though, the process of heading home is much more involved and costly. For many students, going home can cost hundreds of dollars in travel expenses and hundreds more in lost wages that may be involved from missing work. When signing up for any college, you need to consider how far you are away from home and how often you will need to go home as part of your expense of going to college.

If flying is your best option, make sure you check around for the cheapest deal on airfare. However, the cheapest deals might be the biggest hassles with so many restrictions to consider. For instance, you may have many stops and layovers, the layovers may be long, you may only be able to travel on certain days at certain times, you may not be able to travel on weekends, you may have a high penalty to pay for changes, or you may not be entitled to a refund should you cancel. Whenever you book a flight, you need to read the fine print carefully.

To Save Money on Airfare

- Remember prices are higher on the holidays and often during midsummer.

- Look at different airports in the area to see if there is a cheaper alternative to depart or arrive from.

- Check **www.expedia.com**, **www.travelzoo.com**, **www.orbitz.com**, and **www.travelocity.com** to see if you can find a cheap rate.

- Also check on the airlines' own Web sites.

- You might want to talk to a travel agent that specializes in budget travel.

- Find out about red-eye flights.

- Book at least 2 weeks in advance for the best deals.

If you have some time, you might benefit by seeing what a train ride home costs. Find out if Amtrak goes to your area and what a train ride costs by visiting: **www.amtrak. com**.

If you cannot afford to go home often, you could consider staying longer when you do go. That would cut down on travel expenses.

Spring Break

Spring break has its good points — you go off and unwind with your fellow students and have a great time. You might visit a place you have not been to before, perhaps even a foreign country like Mexico or the Bahamas. You might meet life-long friends. You might have the trip of a lifetime; one that you will never forget. However, while spring break is a time to enjoy, you need to be careful and be responsible — for both your personal safety and your money. If you plan on going somewhere, you should consider the following before you book a trip:

- If you are booking through a tour operator, make sure that the organization is reputable and well established. To find out, contact the Student and Youth Travel Association. They describe themselves as "a non-profit, professional trade association whose mission is to promote and support integrity and professionalism among student and youth travel service providers."

Student & Youth Travel Association
3048 Clarkston Road
Lake Orion, MI 48362
800-509-SYTA
www.syta.org

SYTA offers a "Free Travel Safety Tips" brochure on their site, which includes a section on "Questions Parents Should Ask." The brochure is available free of charge on the Web site or by calling the number above.

You can also contact the Better Business Bureau to find out about a tour company.

The Council of Better Business Bureaus
4200 Wilson Blvd, Suite 800
Arlington, VA 22203-1838
703-276-0100
www.bbb.org

When traveling on spring break, or any time, keep in mind these important safety tips:

- When going out, always go out in groups.

- Do not leave your food or drink unattended. Do not accept drinks from strangers. Do not leave intoxicated friends alone.

- Keep your valuables and money locked up in your hotel's safe deposit box. Do not leave your passport and other important documents in your purse or wallet.

- Always wear sunscreen. When lying by the pool

or ocean, you are even more susceptible to burns because of the reflection of sunlight off of the water.

- Do not travel with illegal substances. In a foreign country, you could end up in their prison.

- Avoid casual sex.

The American Medical Association offers these suggestions for how to speak with college kids before a spring break trip. You could use the advice to make your trip safer and less costly:

Top 10 Things to Discuss With Your College Student Before Spring Break

1. Talk to your college student about the health and personal physical safety dangers of excessive alcohol consumption — both by themselves and others (i.e., fighting, drunk driving, and rape).

2. Give your college student tips on how to protect themselves such as traveling in pairs, having money for taxis or public transportation, carrying medical insurance cards and condoms.

3. If your son or daughter is using a tour company to plan their trip, ask to see any promotional materials that helped your college student decide. Make sure that the company is reputable, and that it is not using excessive alcohol promotion to target and influence students.

4. Ask your son or daughter to provide the names and

numbers of any hotels they will be staying in, as well as cell phone numbers for themselves and their friends.

5. Talk to your son or daughter about your expectations and limits with regard to alcohol use.

6. Give them a pre-paid calling card and establish a regular check-in time.

7. Offer to cover the cost of participating in an alternative spring break program.

8. Teach your son or daughter the signs of alcohol poisoning, so that they can better protect their peers and themselves.

9. If your son or daughter is under 21, makes sure that their spring break destination has the same drinking age limitations as do U.S. locations. International locations may allow students as young as 18 to legally purchase alcohol (e.g., Cancun, Mexico).

10. Warn your college student about the danger of drinking and dehydration.

Something you could consider to do instead of traveling for spring break is to create your own spring break without leaving. Instead of spending your hard-earned cash running off to a strange location and opening up the possibilities to get scammed, you could stay close to home and take advantage of what is in your area. For instance, you could spend your week exploring the local parks, enjoying the museums, watching movies, and spending time with your friends. By staying close to home, you will no doubt spend less money than you would traveling, and you may enjoy it just as much. Do not forget your college ID for student discounts.

CASE STUDY: JENNY PHILLIPS

TravelByJen.Com, Inc.

3037 Lawson Blvd, Oceanside, NY 11572

http://www.TravelByJen.Com

info@travelbyjen.com

(800) 603-3178 voice

(516) 594-5788 fax

Jenny Phillips, Owner

Whether college students are heading off to spring break or heading home for the holidays, they can save money on travel by using the right resources and travel agencies that they can trust. TravelByJen.Com is a nationwide agency offering domestic and international vacation and cruise packages. We specialize in discounted space and deal with all types of travel including but not limited to student travel packages and spring break packages. We work with students to find the best deals and the best rates from reputable sources, and the trip enjoyment is tenfold, while the savings can be substantial.

For instance, we had a group of four girls who wanted to go the Oasis Cancun last year — one of the most popular spring break hotels in Cancun — and a competing spring break company was offering a seven-night package for $700 per person for air and hotel (provided that all 4 stayed in the same room). Using a travel consolidator that does over a billion dollars in business in Cancun throughout the year, I was able to get them the same hotel, but the deal I got them was an all-inclusive stay in two rooms for $799 per person. So for $99 per person, they were able to have all their meals and drinks (alcoholic as well), included in the price. The girls each had their own bed and most importantly two bathrooms instead of one.

While you might hear about cheaper deals elsewhere, you might not be happy with what you are getting. At **TravelByJen.Com**, we typically stay away from "spring break tour" companies, because they tend to have less dependable flight arrangements, higher than

CASE STUDY: JENNY PHILLIPS

average problems, and below-average customer service when there are problems. Plus, they try to entice you with exclusive parties and meal deals, but the truth is that these offers are available to everyone or you can forego those options and not be restricted to when and where you eat and drink. Aside from that, their rates on average are higher than normal travel companies. Why does this happen? A spring break tour company only operates for about six weeks per year, so they typically get the lower level of flights, times, and hotel contracts versus a company that will book and operate travel all year round.

If you are looking to save money on airfare home, consider traveling a day or so earlier or later. Airfares are often higher on the weekends and less during the week, so heading home on a Friday and coming back on Monday could be hundreds of dollars cheaper.

Contact us for your travel plans, and we will come up with some affordable options that you will not find just anywhere. After all, not only do we get exclusive inventory that hotels and airlines want to sell at deep discounts, but also, as an agency, we are not obligated to sell only particular airlines or hotels. This means that we can essentially mix and match offers to get the lowest possible rate.

Staying in School

So you have made it through the application process, you have gotten a few scholarships, you have gotten you student loans, figured out your housing and are busy with you studies, but you are feeling frustrated with the workload, overwhelmed with the schedule, and you just cannot figure out how to do your homework assignment. Whatever you do, do not give up and drop out. Your school probably has plenty of resources available to help you ease into school and stick it out until graduation.

If you are unhappy, you need to first figure out what it is that you are unhappy with, for instance:

- If you are having a hard time making friends, try

joining a campus club, or getting a part-time job on campus, which would also put a little extra cash in your pocket.

- If you are struggling with your homework, find out if there is on-campus tutoring available. Even online schools offer tutoring, so there is a good chance you can find help.

- If it is money you are worried about, try getting a part-time job, or keep applying for scholarships and grants. Figure out ways to cut back on your expenses.

- If you do not like your roommate, see if it is possible to switch rooms.

- If you do not like your major, think about switching to another one.

You do not have to sit and be unhappy when there are things you can do to make your school experience so much better, and it pays to stay in school.

According to the Census Bureau's report "College Degree Nearly Doubles Annual Earnings" dated March 28, 2005:

"New information from the U.S. Census Bureau reinforces the value of a college education: workers 18 and over with a bachelor's degree earn an average of $51,206 a year, while those with a high school diploma earn $27,915. Workers with an advanced degree make an average of $74,602, and those without a high school diploma average

$18,734."

Besides a chance to earn higher pay, there are other things to consider, such as the greater ease of attending school while you are younger and do not have as many responsibilities. There is also the social aspect to consider, as people may give a college-degree person more respect, and you might have a better chance of being promoted at work if you have a college degree. So do not drop out, because there are many good reasons to stay in school.

Wrapping It Up

Even if you have received plenty of college funding for tuition and expenses, there are still other expenses that you will incur and need to be considered, such as travel and medical expenses. If you try hard enough you can cut your expenses down in all areas during your college years. Look around for the best deals every time you spend money. Think twice about whether or not you need something. Cutting expenses will lessen what you borrow on loans or borrow on credit cards. If you are considering dropping out of college, think first about why you are unhappy. There is probably a way to make your college years much happier and more productive. College is a big commitment and a big expense, but the payoff is tremendous.

Conclusion

Perhaps you are still pondering whether or not you should proceed with getting your college degree or even finishing it. And you are trying to figure out if all the money, time, and effort pays off in a financial sense. Hopefully it is now clear that with a college degree you still come out way ahead. According to the U.S. Census Bureau's "Educational Attainment in the United States" 2005 report, "...advanced-degree holders made an average of $78,093." That is a lot of income, especially considering that "...those with a high school diploma earned $28,645.... Those without a high school diploma earned an average of $19,169."

When you multiply the $50,000 more per year by the number of years working, getting your college degree makes a whole lot of financial sense.

Forty years working at $50,000 more per year will yield two

million dollars. Even if school costs you $20,000, $30,000 or $40,000 or more to finish, you are still better off.

But what about happiness, you wonder? Does happiness not count? Is it all about money? No, it is not all about money. In addition to potentially providing you with more wealth in your lifetime, having a college degree has been shown to add to your happiness. According to a Pew Research Center survey, "College grads are happier than those without a college degree." Moreover, the Pew Research Center also found that "College-educated adults and high-income adults marry at higher rates and divorce at lower rates than do those with less education and income. They are also less likely to have children outside of marriage."

Even with all the advantages of getting your college degree, when you are just starting on your first year of college, the whole process seems so immense and hard to reach. But like everything else that is worth doing, it takes some dedication and effort.

Let us go through some of the key thoughts that were outlined in this book to put things in perspective.

In Chapter 1, "How Am I Going to Pay for College?," we reviewed ways to pay for school. Remember that you have many options for finishing school, from online education to deciding whether to attend a private or public college or university. By getting an online education you can save money by having the flexibility to work part-time, or you could live in a cheaper state while attending school. You do have choices and ways to cuts costs right from the start.

Chapter 2, "Applications," had us exploring ways to maximize your scholarship potential by beginning as early as high school in your preparations. You can take Advanced Placement courses or work in a community service organization — both of which help on your scholarship application. However, if you did not plan ahead, do not worry, you can still find scholarships and grants that you will be eligible to receive, if you put the effort into finding them. Community college credits are less expensive than what you would pay at a four-year college or university and you get the same degree in the end. Do not give up on finding ways to pay for school, and cutting the costs of school down to minimum.

In Chapter 3, "The Numbers Game," we found useful information on how to apply for the Free Application for Federal Student Aid (FAFSA) in order to generate the Student Aid Report (SAR), which will in turn determine how much money you are going to get. This chapter offers tactics and tips to maximize your benefits. The information was broken down into a process that is easy to understand and full of information to help you fill out your application effectively. With a little time and effort, you can take the first step in getting student loans and scholarships.

Chapter 4, "Grants," examined grants as a way to help cut college expenses. We reviewed the many types of grants that are available and how to get your hands on them. There are many places to look for grants, some of which are in quite surprising locations, such as at local organizations and even through the government. Do not assume one site has everything. Keep looking and you are sure to find grants that you may be eligible to receive.

In Chapter 5, "Learn Now, Pay Later," we covered the many different types of student loans that are available to you and looked over the advantages and disadvantages of them. Yes, you may have to borrow money for school, but with the right loan, you will have low-interest loans that offer some flexibility with repayment.

Chapter 6, "Work It Out!", showed us ways that we could cut expenses by working. We looked at some of the work options that are available to students and how to go about getting the work. Getting your hands dirty may keep your colleges costs down to a minimum. Plus, you will get work experience as you cut your college costs.

In Chapter 7, "The Scholarship Jungle," we explored the many different scholarships available to you, as well as the places you can look for them. We showed you how just about everyone could find a scholarship that they were eligible for if they looked hard enough. Again, a little effort in looking can offer big rewards with what you can receive. Do not stop with one scholarship. You may be eligible for many more.

In Chapter 8, "Bringing It Home," we reviewed how to land the scholarship, as the process is often more extensive than just filling out an application. We covered the steps of acquiring a scholarship, from gathering your transcripts to writing a winning essay to successfully making it through the scholarship interview. By taking the right steps along the way, you will have a better chance of getting the money.

Chapter 9, "Avoiding Trouble," had us exploring some of the ways you do not want to pay for college, such as getting scammed with a bad loan, or falling into other financial disasters. If you keep your eyes open and read the fine print, you will be less likely to be taken advantage of.

Lastly, Chapter 10, "Living Cheap," showed us ways that we could live cheaper while going to school and even after. From getting medical care from healthcare clinics to saving on your trips back home, cutting back on expenses leads to less money that you have to borrow in the first place. It is amazing how many ways you can save, and lower the cost of attending college.

When you think about being able to write your educational background on your resume — B.A., M.A., Ph.D. — as well as increasing your chances of being promoted on the job, and making more money than you would have if you did not finish, and being happier and perhaps healthier, all that time and effort you put into going to college will be well worth it. You will be glad you went ahead and finished your degree, no matter what the cost.

Appendix

The following Web sites may be helpful in your quest to find cash for school. The Web sites were mentioned in the book, but here they are again for your reference. There are plenty more out there.

Colleges and Universities Information

www.co-op.edu National Commission for Cooperative Education.

Guidetoonlineschools.com Am education directory specializing in online degrees, online schools, and distance learning.

www.ncsu.edu North Carolina State University offers cooperative education programs.

www.onlineschools.net Monster's Learning Network includes a source to help you find the right school.

Job Services and Career Advice

www.kellyservices.us Kelly Services provides staffing services and employment opportunities in all states across the U.S.

http://orlandojobspot.blogspot.com Job-hunting tips and employment opportunities.

www.monstertrak.monster.com Monster Trak, career information and job and internship listings.

www.us.manpower.com Manpower, Inc. offers job search by locality and employment resources.

www.vault.com VAULT, Career information and job and internship listings.

Money-Saving Ideas

www.ams.usda.gov/farmersmarkets Find a local farmers market.

www.ask.hrsa.gov/pc U.S. Department of Health and Human Services, Health Resources and Services Administration can help you locate a healthcare center near you.

www.BestWebBuys.com International book deals.

www.bigwords.com Buy and sell textbooks online from student to student.

www.campusbookswap.org Buy and sell textbooks online from student to student.

www.campusbookswap.com Buy and sell textbooks online from student to student.

www.craigslist.com An online want ads that is available in many areas.

www.dentistry.umn.edu University of Minnesota Dental Clinics offer low-cost dental care.

www.farmersmarket.com Find a local farmers market.

www.freecycle.org Check in your area for all kinds of free stuff.

www.FreeDrugDiscountCard.com For savings of up to 75 percent at more than 54,000 national and regional pharmacies.

www.thefrugallife.com Information on how to live frugally with what you have.

www.half.com Buy and sell textbooks online from student to student.

www.iCollegeWeb.com Buy and sell textbooks online from student to student.

www.livingonadime.com Newsletters and articles with money-saving tips.

www.MySavingPlace.com Tips and advice on saving money.

www.textbookx.com Buy and sell textbooks online from student to student.

www.venicefamilyclinic.org Provides free healthcare to low-income patients who lack health insurance.

www.zenhabits.net/2007/08/the-cheapskate-guide-50-tips-for-frugal-living Zen Habits offers a forum to help you save on money by cutting back on expenses.

Organizational Ideas

www.Lifeorganizers.com Organizational tips and resources.

www.CableOrganizer.com Items for your office or home.

Scholarship, Grant and Loan Information and Assistance

www.hbsguru.com The Cambridge Essay Service provides assistance with editing your essays.

www.instantcollegeadmissionessay.com/indexmain.html College Admission Essay Toolkit

www.collegeboard.org Contains information about College Board activities, including AP courses and CLEP exams.

www.essayedge.com The world's largest application essay editing company.

www.fafsa.ed.gov This site has the Web-based version of the FAFSA application.

www.ftc.gov/scholarshipscams A site regarding scholarship scams.

www.gocollege.com A source of information for school funding.

www.finaid.org/calculators Worksheets for estimating EFC.

www.gibill.va.gov Veteran's Administration provides educational benefits for vets.

www.grants.gov The official United States government resource for prospective students offers a free, downloadable handbook to every federal student aid program.

www.instantrecommendationletterkit.com Recommendation letter kit; covers all types of recommendation letters and reference letters including those for college admission and jobs.

www.mapping-your-future.org Mapping Your Future is a public-service, nonprofit Web site providing career, college, financial aid, and financial literacy information and services.

http://moneyforcollege.suntrust.com SunTrust Bank offers student loans and savings programs.

www.oedb.org The Online Education Database is a search engine that contains available college funding state-by-state.

www.oiep.bia.edu Bureau of Indian Affairs offers educational benefits to eligible American Indian/Alaska Native students.

www.srnexpress.com Scholarship Resource Network Express concentrates on scholarships.

www.studentaid.ed.gov The U.S Department of Education's site.

www.studentclearinghouse.org A clearinghouse designed to allow you to order all of your transcripts online.

www.teri.org Find out and apply for a TERI loan.

www.wachovia.com Wachovia Bank offers its Wachovia Individual Education Loan.

Travel

www.amtrak.com Official site for Amtrak passenger trains featuring online reservations, ticket fare finder, trip planning resources, and more.

www.expedia.com Discount travel site.

www.orbitz.com Discount travel site.

www.syta.org The nonprofit, professional trade association that promotes student and youth travel and seeks to foster integrity and professionalism among student and youth travel service providers.

TravelByJen.com Travel agency that also works with students for their travel needs.

www.travelocity.com Discount travel site.

www.travelzoo.com Discount travel site.

Tutoring

www.crowntutoring.com Assistance with studying before major tests such as the SAT and GRE.

Work and Service Programs

www.1800goguard.com The Reserves and the National Guard offer college benefits that you could be entitled to.

www.americorps.gov Americorps provides work opportunities in communities across the country. Upon completion you can apply for a school scholarship.

www.bankofamerica.com Bank of America offers student loan and savings programs.

www.hbsguru.com The Cambridge Essay Service provides essay writing assistance.

www.co-op.edu National Commission for Cooperative Education.

www.gibill.va.gov Veteran's Administration provides educational benefits for vets.

Other

www.us.bbb.org The Better Business Bureaus works to ensure that high standards for businesses are set and maintained.

www.charlim.gather.com Gather is a place to connect with people who share your passions.

www.coachphyllis.com Life coaching and guidance.

www.susan-johnston.com Freelance writer and blogger.

Bibliography

AARP. 2008. **www.aarp.org/about_aarp/nrta/ed_associations**

The American Institute of Certified Public Accountants. 2007. **http://ceae.aicpa.org/Resources/Scholarships+and+Awards/NCCPAP+AICPA+Scholarships.htm**

Aaron, Susan. 2008. The Learning Coach. "Finish That Degree." **www.fastweb.com/fastweb/resources/articles/index/103846**

www.ama-assn.org. "Top 10 Things to Discuss With Your College Student Before Spring Break." Prepared by A Matter of Degree: The National Effort to Reduce High-Risk Drinking Among College Students. Content provided by: Alcohol & Drug Abuse. Mar 28, 2005. **www.ama-assn.org/ama/pub/category/9914.html**

www.associatedcontent.com. "What Should You Consider Before Dropping a College Course? Cutting Your Course Load Can Impact More Than Just Your GPA." M. Pam. Feb 21, 2007. **www.associatedcontent.com/article/149681/what_should_you_consider_before_dropping.html**

Bank of America. 2007. **www.bankofamerica.com**

www.bcsalliance.com. "Get out of Debt by Reducing Monthly Expenses." **www.bcsalliance.com/y_managingyourdebts3.html**

www.bcbs.com. "Study Results Show Medical Expenses Reduced With Preventive Health Program." Egel, Valerie. December 5, 2007. **www.bcbs.com/news/plans/study-results-show-medical.html**

Belluck, Pam. "Harvard, for Less: Extension Courses' New Allure" *The New York Times*, November 18, 2005. **www.nytimes.com/2005/11/18/national/18harvard.html?ei=5088&en=7812fb4a9883e35e&ex=1289970000&partner=rssnyt&emc=rss&pagewanted=all**

California Retired Teachers Association. 2008. **www.calrta.org**

Cardtrack.com. 2008. "Credit Card Debt — What Do Americans Really Owe?" Media Center. **www.cardtrak.com/press/2007.05.31**

www.census.gov. "Census Bureau Data Underscore Value of College Degree." Bergman, Mike. March 28, 2005. **www.census.gov/Press-Release/www/releases/archives/education/004214.html**

College Board. 2007. **www.collegeboard.com**

College Compass. 2007. **www.edonline.com/collegecompass**

College Board's Trends in College Pricing 2007, Trends in Student Aid 2007, and Education Pays. 2007. **www.collegeboard.com/student/pay/add-it-up/4494.html**

DataMasters. **www.datamasters.com**

Education Finance Partners. **www.educationfinancepartners.com/starting_salaries.html**

The Education Resources Institute, Inc. (TERI). 2007. **www.teri.org**

Federal Trade Commission. 2007. **www.ftc.gov/scholarshipscams**

Federal Trade Commission. "Searching for College Money?" September 5, 1996. **www.ftc.gov/opa/1996/09/scholar.shtm**

FindAid. 2007. **www.finaid.org**

www.freecycle.org. 2007. "Mission Statement." **www.freecycle.org/ about/missionstatement**

Get College Scholarships. 2007. "10 Steps Every High School Student Should Take When Preparing for College." **www.get-college-scholar ships.net**

Huddleston, Cameron. "Everything You Need to Know About College Aid: Know the Sources, Learn the Process and Apply Early to Get Your Share of the College Funding Pot of Gold." Kiplinger.com, Feb. 6, 2007. **www.kiplinger.com/features/archives/2007/02/financialaid. html**

J.D. "16 Ways to Eat Healthy While Keeping It Cheap." July, 30 2007. **www.getrichslowly.org/blog/2007/07/30/16-ways-to-eat-healthy-while-keeping-it-cheap/**

Lazarony, Lucy. "Good Deeds Help Pay Down College Debt." Bankrate. com, May 4, 2004. **www.bankrate.com/brm/news/pf/20020215**

"Making Sense of Scholarships: The Ultimate Resource for Successfully Securing College Funding and Grants." 2006. **http://www.ecrater. com/product.php?pid=1553199**

Nellie Mae. A Sallie Mae Student Loan Company. 2007. **www.nelliemae. com/library/scholarships.html**

Nicole, Allen. Textbooks Advocate. "5 Ways to Save on Textbooks Now, 3 Ways to Lower Prices Long Term." August 22, 2007. **www.maketext booksaffordable.org/newsroom.asp?id2=35143**

O'Connor, Tricia, CPA. "How to Dig Yourself Out of Credit Card Debt." *Denver Business Journal.* 4 July, 1997. **www.bizjournals.com/ denver/stories/1997/07/07/smallb4.html?page=2** www.opportunitiesaplenty.com. 2007. "Why Consolidate Your Loans or Other Debt?" **www.opportunitiesaplenty.com/debt_and_loan_ consolidation.html**

Pew Research Center. "Are We Happy Yet?" **www.pewsocialtrends. org/charts/?chartid=29&topicid=5**

Pew Research Center. "As Marriage and Parenthood Drift Apart, Public Is Concerned About Social Impact: Generation Gap in Values, Behaviors." July 1, 2007. **www.pewresearch.org/pubs/526/ marriage-parenthood**

The Project on Student Debt. 2006. **www.projectonstudentdebt.org**

The San Diego Union-Tribune. "Starting Salaries for College Grads." February 20, 2006. **www.signonsandiego.com/uniontrib/20060220/ news_lz1n20thelist.html**

Sanchez, Claudio. "Book Costs Shock College Students, Families." July 25, 2006. **www.npr.org/templates/story/story. php?storyId=5580358**

Singletary, Michelle. 2006. "Books: Colleges' Budget-Busters." Washingtonpost.com, July 13. **www.washingtonpost.com/wp-dyn/ content/article/2006/07/12/AR2006071201979_pf.html**

Stony Brook University. Scholarships, Fellowships & Awards. 2007. **www.sunysb.edu/uaa/scholarshipfellowships/applying.shtml**

Student Aid on the Web. "Loan Consolidation." June 22, 1007. **www. studentaid.ed.gov**

Student Aid on the Web. "Looking for Student Aid...Without Getting Scammed." Sept. 17, 2007. **www.studentaid.ed.gov/ PORTALSWebApp/students/english/lsa.jsp**

Student Youth Travel Association. "Free Travel Safety Tips Brochure." July 13, 2004. **www.syta.org/media.asp?process=view&artID=50**

SunTrust Bank. 2007. **http://moneyforcollege.suntrust.com**

U.S. Census Bureau. 2007. **www.census.gov**

U.S. Department of Education. 2007. U.S. Department of Education. **www.ed.gov**

U.S. Department of Education. 2007. "Loan Consolidation." **www.ed.gov/offices/OSFAP/DCS/consolidation.html**

The Vegetarian Resource Group. 2007. **www.vrg.org/student/scholar.htm**

Wachovia Bank. 2007. **www.wachovia.com**

Weston, Liz Pulliam. 2007. "The Basics: How to Find Free Money for College." MSN Money. **http://articles.moneycentral.msn.com/CollegeAndFamily/CutCollegeCosts/HowToFindFreeMoneyForCollege.aspx**

Wikipedia. "Scholarship." December 19, 2007. **www.en.wikipedia.org/wiki/Scholarship**

Wikipedia. "Stafford Loan." December 5, 2007. **www.en.wikipedia.org/wiki/Stafford_loan**

Witkop, Lori. "Minority Scholarships." 28 June 2006. **http://college.lovetoknow.com/Minority_Scholarships**

www.yale.edu. Adapted from a handout provided by Jane Curlin, Willamette University. "How to Ask for — and Get — Strong Letters of Recommendation." October 9, 2007. **www.yale.edu/iefp/fellowships/other/asking_rec_letters.html**

Author Biography

Ann Marie O'Phelan, M.F.A.

Ann has a B.A. degree in Advertising and Business Management from Metropolitan State University, Minneapolis, and an M.F.A degree in Creative Writing from National University, San Diego, where she graduated with distinction. She worked full-time through all of her schooling, and received merit-based scholarships, and scholarships that were available through local organizations — all helping to reduce her student loans.

Her writing background includes working as an advertising copywriter for notable advertising agencies in Minneapolis, Chicago, and Los Angeles, where she won national and international awards for her work. She currently writes for numerous newspapers and publications, and teaches online writing courses for several universities.

"Pleasure in the job puts perfection in the work."
Aristotle (384 BC – 322 BC)

Index